# Interpreting Music, Engaging Culture

*Interpreting Music, Engaging Culture: An Introduction to Music Criticism* offers a clear, hands-on guide for emerging music critics that brings together aesthetics, critical theory, and practical music criticism in an accessible format. Over the course of the book, readers develop a vocabulary and framework for criticizing music of all kinds and for various media while learning how to connect music to its cultural, social, and political contexts.

Excerpts from primary sources throughout provide a wide range of writing examples, while Chapters address the distinct challenges of describing and interpreting music for various media and in diverse formats. Along the way, the book explores questions at the core of music and its criticism, such as what constitutes a musical work and what makes a piece of music "authentic"; it also introduces critical lenses, including feminist and queer criticism, postcolonialism and critical race theory, as well as the analysis of music in consumer culture. Addressing both classical and popular music criticism, *Interpreting Music, Engaging Culture* is a comprehensive and lively textbook that enables students to uncover, articulate, and analyze what makes music compelling and meaningful.

**Katherine Walker** is Associate Professor of Music at Hobart & William Smith Colleges.

# Interpreting Music, Engaging Culture
## An Introduction to Music Criticism

Katherine Walker

NEW YORK AND LONDON

Designed cover image: Nikolay Tsuguliev

First published 2025
by Routledge
605 Third Avenue, New York, NY 10158

and by Routledge
4 Park Square, Milton Park, Abingdon, Oxon, OX14 4RN

*Routledge is an imprint of the Taylor & Francis Group, an informa business*

© 2025 Taylor & Francis

The right of Katherine Walker to be identified as author of this work has been asserted in accordance with sections 77 and 78 of the Copyright, Designs and Patents Act 1988.

All rights reserved. No part of this book may be reprinted or reproduced or utilised in any form or by any electronic, mechanical, or other means, now known or hereafter invented, including photocopying and recording, or in any information storage or retrieval system, without permission in writing from the publishers.

*Trademark notice*: Product or corporate names may be trademarks or registered trademarks, and are used only for identification and explanation without intent to infringe.

ISBN: 978-1-138-58559-1 (hbk)
ISBN: 978-1-138-58560-7 (pbk)
ISBN: 978-0-429-50517-1 (ebk)

DOI: 10.4324/9780429505171

Typeset in Sabon
by Apex CoVantage, LLC

This book is dedicated to the family I made and the family I chose:
Clara, Eme, Ian, and Rhys

# Contents

*How to Use This Book*     xi

**Introduction: A Critical Engagement With Music**     1
   *Critical Discourse* 2
   *From Critical to Criticism* 3
   *What's Not Criticism?* 14
   *Why Do Criticism?* 15
   *Chapter Summary* 16

### PART 1
**Aesthetic Foundations**     19

**1   What Is Art? The Musical Work Problem**     21
   *The Musical Work Concept* 21
   *Getting to Know the Musical Work* 25
   *Historically Informed Performance (HIP) Movement* 25
   *Getting to Know Technical Aspects of the Performance* 28
   *Getting to Know Interpretive Aspects of the Performance* 29
   *The Musical Work and Value* 30
   *The Case of Popular Music* 31
   *Chapter Summary* 36

**2   Music and Authenticity**     38
   *Defining Authenticity* 39
   *Folk Authenticity* 41
   *Authenticity in Hip-Hop* 45
   *Chapter Summary* 50

## 3 Beyond Authenticity 53
*Postmodernism 53*
*Postmodern Music and Its Criticism 56*
*Postmodernism in a Post-Truth Era 63*
*Chapter Summary 65*

## PART 2
# Criticizing Music 67

## 4 Describing Music 69
*Elements of Music 74*
*Genre 80*
*Style Period 82*
*Audience 83*
*Chapter Summary 83*

## 5 Interpreting Music 86
*Musical Interpretation 88*
*Interpretive Strategies 94*
*Chapter Summary 95*

## 6 Evaluating Music 98
*Some Negative Criticism of Negative Criticism 98*
*Evaluation and the Work's Purpose 100*
*The Value of the Purpose 104*
*The Critic as Educator 106*
*Chapter Summary 108*

## PART 3
# Critical Lenses 111

## 7 Feminist Music Criticism 113
*Feminism and Feminisms 113*
*Why Do We Need Feminism? 114*
*History of Feminisms 115*
*Feminism and Music 116*
*Feminist Criticism 119*
*Chapter Summary 123*

| | | |
|---|---|---|
| 8 | **Queer Music Criticism** | 126 |
| | *Genderqueer 127* | |
| | *Queering the Patriarchy 129* | |
| | *Music and Queer Expression 130* | |
| | *Camp Isn't Always Queer 131* | |
| | *Queer Isn't Always Camp 134* | |
| | *Queer Criticism as History and Allyship 138* | |
| | *Chapter Summary 139* | |
| 9 | **Postcolonialism and Critical Race Theory** | 141 |
| | *Orientalism 142* | |
| | *Postcolonialism 144* | |
| | *Postcolonialism and Critical Race Theory 147* | |
| | *Chapter Summary 152* | |
| 10 | **Music and Consumer Culture** | 154 |
| | *The Case of Popular Music 155* | |
| | *Embedded Advertising in Popular Music 157* | |
| | *Music and Marketing in the Age of Social Media 159* | |
| | *Chapter Summary 162* | |

**PART 4**
**Critical Contexts** 165

| | | |
|---|---|---|
| 11 | **Album and Track-by-Track Reviews** | 167 |
| | *Album Review in the Age of Streaming 167* | |
| | *Track-by-Track Review 171* | |
| | *Writing for a Specific Publication 174* | |
| | *Chapter Summary 175* | |
| 12 | **Program Notes and the Live Concert Review** | 178 |
| | *Program Notes as Guide 178* | |
| | *Live Review 182* | |
| | *Chapter Summary 189* | |

*Index* 191

# How to Use This Book

**For Students**

A book about music criticism is, at its heart, a book about music. The reviews in this book span a wide range of genres, styles, and even time periods. You will read about Bach and Beethoven; the Pixies and PJ Harvey; Taylor Swift and Nicki Minaj; and Arcade Fire and Radiohead. For these critics, and for me, the reviews are intended to be companion pieces to the music itself. In order to benefit fully from the content of this book, be sure to listen to the music that is the subject of the review at hand. (You may wish to experiment with listening before and after reading the review. Does it shape or influence the listening experience?) Watch the videos when relevant and pull up the lyrics alongside any critical discussion of them.

Sometimes, in the service of space or for reasons of copyright, only a short passage of a review is quoted in the book. In such instances, I encourage you to refer to the entire review whenever possible. Many of the reviews in this book are quoted from open-access websites like *Pitchfork*, *The Quietus*, *Boston Classical Review*; other sources, like *The New York Times* and *The San Francisco Chronicle*, may be available through your public or academic library system. Similarly, pulling up the lyrics or a song's accompanying music video, whenever relevant, will enrich your understanding of the content at hand.

Lastly, while the book focuses on music criticism, it contains so much more—you'll be introduced to critical theory, popular culture studies, history, aesthetics, and music theory. Indeed, any one of the chapters in this book could be its own book; some of them could be entire libraries. If you feel drawn in by a topic raised in the book, please know that there is a whole universe of knowledge and interest awaiting you. Consider taking a course in critical theory or reading books devoted specifically to feminism or aesthetics. This broad overview provides access to many different disciplines and epistemologies. I hope that you will travel further down the road with some of them.

## For Instructors

The 13 chapters of this book roughly align to a 16-week semester (when accounting for final projects, exams, and breaks). Nevertheless, the pacing through the chapters is not a steady one. Some topics are introduced in this book that deserve more attention than suggested by the space I give them. For example, although I have devoted only a few paragraphs to the concept of taste, I teach an entire unit on that topic in my Aesthetics course. As you organize your syllabus and prepare to teach this material, I invite you to consider where you might want to pull in the reins, add additional readings, and go deeper into a topic.

Although the book contains some music terminology, including references to the backbeat, time signatures, appoggiaturas, etc., those references generally accompany explanations; and students can most certainly engage the material without being literate in them. There is no need to require music theory prerequisites for a student's engagement with this book. On the contrary, the book has utility well beyond the realm of academic music studies; it may be an appropriate resource for a course on journalism, popular culture studies, media studies, and nonfiction writing. It can also provide an accessible alternative to traditional *Introduction to Music* textbooks.

As stated in the "For Students" section, above, I encourage you and your students to refer to the entire review when only a short excerpt is quoted. Many can be found on open-access websites or (as is the case with *The New York Times*, for example) through your academic library system. Engaging with the entire review will enhance student learning and enrich the topic at hand. Lastly, though it goes without saying, the music itself is the primary source material of this book and should be at the center of the student's engagement with it.

# Introduction
## A Critical Engagement With Music

Imagine that you are walking down the street, listening to music through your ear buds, as Katy Perry's pop anthem "Roar" begins to play. Your gait changes imperceptibly as you pace yourself to the beat. Your head starts to move with the music, and your mouth forms the words along with the singer. As the climactic chorus approaches, your fingers instinctively reach for the volume button on the side of your phone (though it's already playing at the maximum level). When the long-awaited chorus drops, your arms swing freely by your side, and your step becomes bouncy and rhythmic. Now you're outright singing along as the music washes over you: "I've got the eye of the tiger, the dah dah, something something fire, 'cause I am a champion . . ." You glance ahead and see someone smiling at you. You realize at that moment that, not only have you been putting on your own one-person show, the show is pretty bad. How can it be that you don't know the lyrics to a song that you have heard so many times?

Suppose this question gnaws at you, and you find yourself looking up the lyrics later that day. Scanning the text, you are struck by how few lyrics there are. You are familiar with the standard verse-chorus pop song structure; here, each chorus is preceded by a "pre-chorus," which (like the chorus) restates its own lyrics and music. The verses seem diminutive and insignificant in relation to the repeating, multi-section chorus, which occupies so much of the song. In fact, you notice that the verses gradually diminish in length as the song unfolds. The first verse contains two parallel statements of three phrases each. The second verse (which begins, "Now I'm floating") only has one such statement, rendering it half as long as the previous verse. Following the second statement of the chorus is a mere shadow of a verse, a brief transition section, which recalls themes from the chorus, itself. One does not have to wait long for the third, extended statement of the chorus, which brings the song to its exultant, highly satisfying conclusion.

Listening to the song confirms your observation. The space occupied by verses gradually decreases, propelling the music forward, toward each culminating statement of the chorus. It's almost as if this song can be reduced

DOI: 10.4324/9780429505171-1

to music that anticipates the chorus and the chorus, itself. Now you understand why the lyrics have eluded you all this time; the arrival of the chorus is so immersive that it leaves little room for reflection. And yet that sense of abandon, of losing oneself in the music, is precisely what makes the song so satisfying to listen to. You put your ear buds back in, and, setting aside for the moment thoughts of compressed forms and extended choruses, you lose yourself in the music, enjoying the emotions it conjures and the movement that it generates in your body. As the chorus drops, you sing the lyrics, this time, not missing a word.

This is a story about two ways of listening to music, the first of which is probably familiar to you. Even if you've never sung your way down the street with your ear buds in, you've probably enjoyed the pleasures of dancing to music or the boost that an upbeat song can provide to an exercise regime. For most of us, in these contexts, it's as if the body has its own way of comprehending musical meaning. Our experience is immersive, embodied, and ultimately passive.[1] In the story above, however, you temporarily stepped out of that passive, embodied state to actively engage with the music. You asked questions, made observations, and drew meaningful conclusions about its structure and form. Although you didn't publish your ideas on a music website; though you're not preparing a lecture on the compressed form of Katy Perry's "Roar"; though you haven't even made any judgments about the value of the song, you have nonetheless enacted a shift from passive and embodied to active and reflective engagement with music. That shift marks the beginning of criticism as this book defines it.

### Critical Discourse

The word *criticism* originates from Greek, *kritikos*, meaning "to judge" or "to decide." Given its etymology, it may be no wonder that criticism is often disparaged as being explicitly evaluative and implicitly negative. In practice, however, criticism encompasses a great deal more than judgment. Broadly speaking, it is a form of discourse, in that it produces and reinforces systematic ways of actively engaging a subject through language. It thus follows that music criticism involves the use of language to actively engage with musical sounds and contexts. Such engagement may include describing a song (album, band, genre, or performance), interpreting its meaning, analyzing its structure and composition, evaluating its worth, and/or placing it in its proper historical or cultural context. To engage with music critically is, in this broad sense, to engage with it discursively; that is, actively and systematically, through language.

Viewed in this way, you probably encounter music criticism regularly in your everyday life. Certainly, an album review published in *Rolling Stone* magazine constitutes music criticism. However, have you considered that the informal debate that you had with a friend over which band is better is also a critical activity? A piano teacher who encourages a student to approach a piece of music from a certain interpretive or stylistic perspective; a music major who writes a paper on Debussy; even a person contemplating the unfolding structure of Katy Perry's "Roar," is engaged in music-critical work. The differences between these various critical activities relate to the degree and kinds of knowledge that each person possesses and the purposes to which the knowledge is put. Knowledge strengthens a critical voice and directs it toward certain observations and conclusions.

In the Katy Perry example above, one needs certain habits of listening and knowledge of music in order to perceive the gradual compression of the verses. One must be able to distinguish between a verse, pre-chorus, and chorus, and be able to count musical phrases in the respective sections. It also helps to understand tempo and meter and to be able to count beats and measures. Indeed, the more knowledge one possesses, the more equipped they are to engage in meaningful critical work. Knowledge, however, is not linear; it can expand in any number of directions, such that different kinds of knowledge point the critical engagement toward different conclusions. A computer scientist who makes beats in their spare time might notice the conspicuous absence of a backbeat until the onset of the chorus. The political theorist, meanwhile, might investigate Hillary Clinton's promotional use of this song during her 2016 presidential campaign. The women's studies major might be interested in the music video, reflecting on the complexities and contradictions of mainstream pop culture's particular shade of feminism. Each of these modes of inquiry is valid, for there is no single answer to the question of a song's meaning.

## From Critical to Criticism

As suggested, critical discourse involves the use of language to understand and provide understanding about music and its contexts. Thus defined, critical discourse encompasses a vast array of activities, spanning diverse disciplines and professions (both within and outside of music). Criticism begins with critical discourse, applying its methods to specific goals and outcomes. Here again, the scope of activities and priorities is vast; nevertheless, music critics are, on the whole, concerned with a category of questions that distinguish them from other writers on music, and they frame their answers in discipline-specific ways. While there is no universal agreement about the parameters or definition of music criticism, the following general guidelines may distinguish music criticism from other related activities.

**Critics are concerned with present-day music and music culture.**

This is not to say that critics don't write about music composed in the past; on the contrary, much present-day concert life is centered on the historical canon. However, criticism primarily concerns present-day music culture and the music—be it ancient or contemporary—that contributes to it.

Consider this essay by William Robin, a music critic for *The New Yorker*.[2] It begins with a clear grounding in history:

> Over the course of eight weeks, the group of passionate London musicians mounted the first-ever survey of Beethoven's sixteen string quartets. The Society distributed scores for dedicated audience members to peruse; attendees were asked to arrive thirty minutes early so as not to disrupt the music.

In this brief introductory paragraph, the reader is transported to nineteenth-century London, where erudite concertgoers rustled scores in an otherwise hushed auditorium, awaiting another performance of Beethoven's string quartets. Yet just as swiftly as the reader was transported into the past, they are pulled back into the present:

> That spirit of veneration has changed very little. Today, cycles of Beethoven's quartets, symphonies, and piano sonatas are ubiquitous. Up-and-coming string quartets frequently take a crack at performing the complete Beethoven. A traversal of the composer's nine symphonies has become a regular staple of the concert hall.

As the essay unfolds, the author moves fluidly between the past and the present, focusing in turn on Beethoven's lifetime, his later nineteenth-century legacy, and current trends in performing and recording his music. Notwithstanding this fluidity, the purpose of the essay—its thesis and conclusion—concerns present-day music culture:

> The benefits of listening to a full set of sonatas, symphonies, or quartets are obvious: they paint a rich portrait of a composer's musical development, allowing connections to be heard across an artistic career. [. . .] For the interpreter, cycles offer an opportunity to grapple with repertoire on a grand scale. [. . .]
> 
> Yet, there is something puzzling about the classical fixation on cycles. Unlike Wagner's "Ring" or Schubert's "Winterreise," Beethoven's sonatas do not tell a singular, unified story. The composer did not know that he would write a ninth symphony when he composed his first. These omnipresent cycles represent, instead, an anachronistic grouping— one made only in hindsight and informed by a shrewd combination

of the Romantic ethos of classical music and the box-set mentality of the record industry. And, though they claim to embrace a wide swath of music, cycles are symptomatic of the past century's thinning of the repertory, one that has squeezed out much fascinating music and left behind only the most pre-sanctioned of classics.

Ultimately, this essay posits a critique of a commodified record industry, a shrinking canon, and an anachronistic Romantic ethos of classical music. The author reaches expertly into the past in order to bring light to present-day music culture. Focus on the present is a basic tenet of this piece and of music criticism in general.

**Critics operate in the subjective realm of taste.**

Criticism has been designated "history without footnotes," which reflects the commonplace frustration with writing that is at once persuasive and informative and, at the same time, unsubstantiated by scholarly methods.[3] Even with its footnotes, history (like any discipline) takes shape in part through the priorities, goals, and thought processes of the historians that write it. In fact, an entire subdiscipline, historiography, exists to interrogate the claims, biases, and agendas that underwrite our historical narratives. While history's authors tend to recede into the background of their writings, historiography situates them in the foreground and makes visible the fact that history is written in and for the present; that it is, essentially, a story.

In this sense, criticism and history are analogous: each provides a lens—framed and focused by its authors—through which to experience a particular object or event. Nevertheless, there is an important difference between the disposition of the historian and that of the critic: the historian seeks to attenuate bias and takes as a professional goal the maintenance of maximum personal distance from the subject; the critic, on the other hand, invites the reader directly into their subjective point of view.

Consider Laurie Anderson's review of Animal Collective's album, *Centipede HZ*[4]:

> First of all, I hate to admit it but you might as well know it right off: the more it sounds like "Grass" (my favorite Animal Collective song) the more I like it.
> 
> "Grass" is ecstatic. A huge football game that goes haywire. The players suddenly running in circles, insanely chirping cartoon birds, clouds billowing, the marching band spelling out arcane words in quickly shifting formations, the scoreboard in fast forward, the crowd going "Rah! Rah! Rah! Rah! Rah! Rah!"

> As a musician I know that's not the most generous approach to a new record that has ambitions and lots of great sounds and dangerous harmonies and new constructions. It's not fair to hope it sounds like something from the past. But I just can't help it. "Grass" is so full of joy and freedom, all that manic humming and rattling and chirping. Are there more of you out there like that?

Not only are her first-person voice and colloquial, almost confessional, tone acceptable in the realm of criticism (as opposed to an historical essay, where they may be out of place), they are standard in the field. Indeed, the reader expects to meet with the subjective impressions of the critic. For contemporary music and literary critic R. J. Wheaton, a critic needs

> taste . . . [Y]ou need to have an opinion on which types of music, which artists, which techniques are better than others. You need to have an opinion on why. And you need to be able to explain or imply that in a compelling and interesting way. Without that, your writing will lack passion and you yourself will lack the drive to explore the new, whether it's actually new or merely new to you in the service of deepening your enthusiasms.[5]

Of course, taste cannot be reduced to opinion alone, as Wheaton seems to suggest. This complex concept is a central preoccupation of the philosophy of art, among whose earliest and most probing examiners was the eighteenth-century German philosopher Immanuel Kant. For Kant, taste is a faculty of judgment, which responds to feelings of pleasure or displeasure when experiencing an aesthetic object (usually an object of art or nature). Whereas the rightness of a mathematical principle can be logically defended, the value of a symphony or a painting is determined by the pleasure that it awakens in the perceiver. Judgments of taste, thus based on feelings of pleasure and displeasure, are necessarily subjective.

In matters of taste, however, subjectivity is not to be confused with personal preferences and predilections. Aesthetic pleasure denotes a specific kind of subjectivity because it is "disinterested," which, for Kant, means that it is divorced from desire. Compare, for example, the pleasure derived from experiencing a sunset with that derived from a cookie. We can enjoy a sunset without wanting anything from it, but the perception of a cookie activates our appetitive motives and responses. Examining this distinction more closely, we observe that it is not the sunset itself but its representation that pleases us—its colors, shapes, and movements. The cookie, on the other hand, offers something beyond its representation—namely, calories. (To focus on the light and warmth provided by the sun would similarly be to turn away from the aesthetic.) Thus subjectivity, as a feature of taste, refers to the disinterested pleasure (or displeasure) experienced in perceiving the *representation* of an aesthetic object.

Subjectivity is the first of two essential features of Kant's formulation of taste. The second is, somewhat paradoxically, universality. Aesthetic responses seem to derive from properties of the objects themselves, and, as such, seem to transcend individual preferences to communicate universal truths. Universality suggests that the perceiver feels "as if beauty were a property of the object" and not a feature of one's experience.[6] Thus, we tend to believe that sunsets, for example, give pleasure because they are innately beautiful and not because we subjectively perceive them as such. Although the language of "seeming" and "believing" is necessarily tentative, a wealth of universally appreciated art confirms the mysterious logic of subjective universality. The beauty of a Bach sonata or Shakespeare sonnet cannot be logically defended because it rests on subjective pleasure; yet that pleasure is so widely shared that it seems to transcend our subjective impressions to communicate something universally true. Indeed, if I don't care for a particular food or type of weather, you will not question my taste, but if I don't care for a Bach sonata or Shakespeare sonnet, you will believe that I am wrong. Kant describes this feature of aesthetic judgment in no uncertain terms:

> If [a person] pronounces that something is beautiful, then he expects the very same satisfaction of others: he judges not merely for himself, but for everyone, and speaks of beauty as if it were a property of things. Hence he says that the thing is beautiful, and does not count on the agreement of others with his judgment of satisfaction because he has frequently found them to be agreeable with his own, but rather demands it from them. He rebukes them if they judge otherwise, and denies that they have taste, though he nevertheless requires that they ought to have it; and to this extent one cannot say, "Everyone has his special taste." This would be as much as to say that there is no taste at all, i.e., no aesthetic judgment that could make a rightful claim to the assent of everyone.[7]

The claim to universality is a keystone of aesthetic judgment and a distinction between personal preferences and judgments of taste. It is marked by a shift in focus from properties in the perceiver (e.g., "I like this painting because red is my favorite color") to features of the object itself (e.g., "The reds in this painting have tremendous depth").

Despite Anderson's initially subjective first-person praise of "Grass" in the review above, the essay unfolds to emphasize features in the music as opposed to resting on her personal preferences and predilections:

> Centipede Hz is a record with lots of things in it—motors and propellers, a giant samba band with the massive surdo drum. A record that's going somewhere, inventing its own form of transportation.
>
> And it's in the transitions where you can hear the method, the sounds of large structures breaking down into pieces, chunks, the metal springs

still trembling, the spent batteries. And it's from these pieces that are lying around that the next song is swiftly deftly assembled. In "Pulleys" the initial construction is half techno, half organic. Big bundles of hollow rushes through Indonesian filters mix with big, thick chords and a massive, pointy bass line, hooting smoky vocals that curl and twist. Once in a while a vocoder.

By the end of the review, we've traveled a significant distance from Anderson's almost confessional opening lines that communicated her love for "Grass." Her comments are now firmly rooted in the music, as she turns our attention from the fact that she likes the album to the reasons why. We may not have listened to the album, but we hear it nonetheless: it is nostalgically industrial, with big, machine-like motives that are made to dance over Latin rhythms; it contains short, metallic ideas that are presented and then swiftly dissembled and reconfigured as if they were Legos; and one hears non-western exoticisms and big, earthy drums alongside the eerie crooning of a vocoder. Anderson's description vividly captures the energy and excitement of the album, the irreverent mix of nostalgic and new, urban and rural, western and other. Though her review begins by emphasizing her personal preferences, it ultimately provides the reader with a compelling justification for her judgments.

Reflecting now on the opening lines, which initially seemed so subjective, it is clear that the first-person language and ironically apologetic tone provided a foil for her critical evaluations. Critical judgments are judgments of taste, which, while subjective, are nevertheless justified by qualities that inhere in the work of art (rather than qualities, experiences, and preferences of the perceiver), and by means of these justifications demand universal agreement.

So far, so good. Why, then, did Salvador Dali proclaim that "it is good taste, and good taste alone, that possesses the power to sterilize and is always the first handicap to any creative functioning"? Why did Pablo Picasso cite "good taste" as "the enemy of creativeness"? And why did George Bernard Shaw define a "man of great common sense and good taste" as "thereby a man without originality or moral courage"?

First of all, these artists recognized that taste tends to favor established (over emerging) aesthetic ideals. This is perhaps one reason why the term avant-garde so aptly describes artists on the forefront of their respective mediums. A medieval French military term, "avant-garde" (literally, "advance guard") originally referred to soldiers on the front line of an advancing military formation. The avant-garde were the first to deploy in battle, and as such the first to meet with opposition. In the early twentieth century, the term was repurposed for artists and works that promoted new, experimental ideas. This connotation communicates both the broad cultural significance of experimentation, as well as the tremendous opposition to it. Dali, Picasso, and others associated such opposition with guardians of "good taste," who held stubbornly to entrenched aesthetic values. Music history can provide any number of examples of the tension between good taste and good emerging art. To provide but one, the opening-night performance of Igor Stravinsky's Russian ballet *Le Scare du printemps* (The Rite of Spring) in 1913, by all accounts, incited a cacophony of dissent. Among many such protests, one critic saw the work as a joke, and one moreover that "was not in very good taste."[8] Today, this groundbreaking work is considered one of the great masterpieces in the western musical canon, suggesting that good art and good taste are not always in synchrony.

Secondly, scholars observe that distinctions of taste often operate alongside distinctions of class and that a refined taste for high art can provide social capital for those who identify (or wish to identify) as elite. The aspirational tendencies of good taste support a false dichotomy between art and entertainment, elevating the former, while inadvertently undermining its entertainment value. Richard Taruskin, a contemporary musicologist and music critic, vividly captures this problem as it pertains to classical music. In surveying the so-called crisis of classical music consumption through books devoted to this topic, Taruskin observes a discouraging trend: defenders of classical music inadvertently supported its status as elite and exclusive:

> The discourse supporting classical music so reeks of historical blindness and sanctimonious self-regard as to render the object of its ministrations practically indefensible. Belief in its indispensability, or in its cultural superiority, is by now unrecoverable, and those who mount such arguments on its behalf morally indict themselves.[9]

For Taruskin, devotees of classical music would do better to cast it as populist and accessible so that it may be more widely enjoyed.

There are lessons in both of these considerations. At their best, judgments of taste succumb neither to entrenched aesthetic values nor to aspirational prejudices. Rather, they emphasize qualities that inhere in the work and use deliberate, reliable measures of value.

**Critics are knowledgeable about music.**

Art historian Edmund Feldman describes criticism as "informed talk about art."[10,11] Being informed means knowing about the music, musicians, composers and creators, audiences, performances, and cultural and historical contexts around which music is created and consumed.

This may sound onerous, but much useful information about music is commonly known. Even if you hear soaring strings in an Adele song, you will probably not confuse it with classical music. You can probably identify the difference between the standard drum kit used in rock 'n' roll and West African cowbells and hand drums. You know not to judge a Haydn symphony based on how danceable it is, nor would you criticize a rap lyricist for using improper grammar. You may be able to tell the difference between an opera and a musical or between a symphony and a big band orchestra. If you go to a jazz club, you probably expect the musicians to improvise. You may be able to recognize the sounds of some common instruments, such as the piano, guitar, drums, and bass. Perhaps you know a great deal more. Regardless of where you are on the journey of acquired musical literacy, you bring knowledge, habits, and experiences that inform your critical work.

For the outspoken literary critic, Noël Carroll, determining a work's meaning and value emerges from an understanding of its purpose. Carroll's argument invites us to consider that Katy Perry has an entirely different purpose than, say, Mozart did; and that it would be ludicrous to judge them based on the same criteria. For Carroll, the purpose of a work, and therefore the criteria for judgment, are partly reflected in categories:

> Fundamental to the task of criticism is placing the artwork at hand in its proper category (or categories), because once we know the category (or categories) to which the artwork belongs, we have a sense of the kind of expectations that it is appropriate to bring to the work."[12]

In music, categories are primarily organized around genre, style period, and audience. These categories provide a framework for examining the purpose of a musical work in a meaningful, appropriate way. We can all agree that it makes no sense to compare Katy Perry to Mozart; they had different aims, and their music works on us in different ways. However, the music critic observes further distinctions between Katy Perry and, for example, Yes, a popular progressive rock group, which nevertheless held high artistic pretensions that transcended mass appeal. Chapter 4 addresses these elements—genre, style period, and audience—in more detail. A small degree of articulation suffices here:

### Genre

Genre refers to a system of categorizing cultural artifacts (such as musical groups and works) according to shared stylistic features, forms, performance contexts, traditions, and values. Some generally recognized genres of music are country, rap, pop, rock, jazz, classical, alternative, and punk.

Each of these genres can be further divided into subgenres. Within classical music, subgenres include opera, art song, symphony, and chamber music. Within jazz, subgenres include bebop, big band, free jazz, and hard bop. Understanding the conventions and stylistic features of individual genres (and subgenres) provides an important fund of knowledge for interpreting and evaluating musical works.

*Style Period*

Style period refers to the historical moment in which the work was created and/or experienced and the artistic conventions that proliferated in that moment. In some cases, the style period corresponds to the genre. The development of jazz, for example, is very much tied to historical era: the "swing era" refers both to the 1930s and to the big band style of dance-oriented jazz that prevailed in that period. In other cases, however, style period and genre are mutually exclusive. Though they are both pop stars, it makes little sense to compare Cindy Lauper to Taylor Swift. They are each artists of their own time, with their own priorities and musical means available to them. Similarly, it would be inappropriate to compare the heavy vibrato of a Handel aria recording from the 1920s with the crisp and airy sound of a more contemporary recording of the same piece.

*Audience*

Who is the intended audience for a particular work or performance? A piece written for mass consumption, radio play, and streaming culture will be entirely different from a piece that is meant to be performed for a small, initiated audience in an art house. Considering the consumption goals of a piece provides an important lens for determining its purpose and meaning.

**Critical evaluations can be organized into distinct schools of thought.**

Interpretations of and judgments about art cannot be divorced from cultural factors; a critic's gender identity, socioeconomic status, ethnicity, education, upbringing, life experiences, and values, etc., inevitably shape their critical responses in sometimes predictable and consistent ways. Values in particular may cohere into distinct critical systems; they can become frameworks for interpreting and evaluating art, which reflect a commitment to a specific belief system. There are multiple, sometimes competing, critical systems, each with its own vocabulary, expressions, and perspectives and, beneath these, agendas, biases, and points of view. Some of these have a decidedly political bent. Part Three of this book examines four critical systems in detail. These systems—feminism, queer theory, postcolonial theory, and capitalist critique—are briefly introduced here.

## *Feminism*

Feminism refers to the ongoing struggle for economic, social, political, and cultural equality for women. Broadly defined, it encompasses competing and in some cases contradictory agendas, concerns, and priorities throughout history and across diverse world cultures. There is no such thing as a unified feminism, and likewise no single definition of feminist art. On the contrary, its terms and characteristics are highly contested. For example, some feminists celebrate the controversial female rapper Nicky Minaj; others see her as anathema to their feminist agenda. Disagreements such as that should be seen to reflect the richness and diversity of contemporary feminisms, as well as the varied forms that women's rights can and must take. Furthermore, despite their disparate lenses, all feminist artists and critics share an acknowledgment of the ongoing oppression of women and a commitment to eradicating it by politicizing art and its discourses.

Since the Civil Rights period, black feminists, including, notably, Alice Walker and Angela Davis, have argued that sexism is intertwined with racism, classism, and heterosexism. Intersectionality, the acknowledgment of the deep-seated connections between distinct forms of cultural oppression, informs contemporary feminisms.

## *Queer Theory*

Queer theory makes visible and interrogates normative assumptions about gender and sexuality as well as their various manifestations in the cultural, social, economic, and political arenas. Like feminism (with which queer theory shares foundational ideas and agendas), queer theory encompasses a wide range of priorities, values, and concerns, including the normative dichotomy between homosexual and heterosexual (and between masculine and feminine), perceived "mismatches between sex, gender, and desire,"[13] and the relative presence or absence of infrastructures that support identity- and sexuality-diversity. As with the other systems, art can project, promote, or critique issues associated with gender and sexual identity.

## *Postcolonial and Critical Race Theory*

Postcolonialism is a multi- and inter-disciplinary area of study that is concerned with the economic, social, and cultural situations of people and nations that have existed under colonialist or hegemonic power structures. Postcolonialism is rooted in the work of Edward Said, a Palestinian-born professor of literature at Columbia University, whose seminal book *Orientalism* (1978) examines construction of the so-called Orient in the Western imagination. *Orientalism* focuses on the colonialist mindset that underwrites many Western depictions of the "other," broadly conceived. Critical race theory shares many values and priorities with postcolonialism but emerged from the post-Civil Rights era experience of people of color in the United States. According to Kimberlé Crenshaw, CRT

> is a way of seeing, attending to, accounting for, tracing and analyzing the ways that race is produced,°.°.°. the ways that racial inequality is facilitated, and the ways that our history has created these inequalities that now can be almost effortlessly reproduced unless we attend to the existence of these inequalities.[14]

Like images and words, musical sounds can transmit concepts of East and West, Black and White, self and other, right and wrong and can therefore intersect with Postcolonial and Critical Race Theories.

*Capitalist Critique*

In the nineteenth century, Karl Marx and his collaborator Friedrich Engels developed a political-economic theory that has had a wide-reaching impact on thinkers in economics, politics, philosophy, aesthetics, history, the arts, and other disciplines. Marxists argued that capitalism legitimizes a class-divided society, such that an elite minority owns the means of production, and an exploited majority works for wages. The alienation experienced by wage laborers (who have no stake in the integrity of the product) thus transcends the economic sphere to impact the other aspects of society. At its most extreme, capitalism subsumes culture itself:

> Culture does not emerge from the free creative expression of social agents but is constructed in commodity form by an alliance of the state and private corporations. It signals the complete rationalization of the emancipatory powers of creativity, where creativity is converted into standardized mass-produced products and reduced to basic formulaic patterns of taste. This commercialized culture engenders intellectual passivity and docility, which themselves are the conditions needed for authoritarian politics to reign.[15]

For many, the problems and tensions raised by Marx, Engels, and their colleagues in the nineteenth-century resonate today. Musical works can treat these problems and tensions as their subject matter. They can be created through forces that are subject to capitalist critique, making them a symptom of broader social and economic problems. They can also project images (either true or false) of capitalism and commodity culture.

**Critics enhance present-day music culture and provide a bridge between music and its public.**

Music criticism, at its best, transmits appreciation and respect for the art form and thus fosters enthusiasm for its experience. As American art critic Rosalind Krauss suggests,

> presumably one gets involved with this rather particular, rather esoteric form of expression because one has had some kind of powerful experience with it—and presumably this powerful experience then makes you want to go on and think about it and learn about it and write about it. But you must have at some point been ravished, been seduced, been taken in.[16]

For Noël Carroll, similarly,

> the primary function of the critic is not to eviscerate artworks. Rather, I hypothesize that the audience typically looks to critics for assistance in discovering the value to be had from the works under review . . . . [T]he critic also occupies a social role. In that social role, the primary function of criticism is to enable readers to find the value that the critic believes that the work possesses. It is the task of criticism to remove any obstacles that might stand in the way of the reader's apprehension of that value.[17]

This is not to suggest that there is no place for negative criticism. However, like all communication, criticism—whether positive or negative—should be respectful, honest, and purposeful. It should reflect open-mindedness and a desire to advance the art form under discussion. Negative criticism, when truly called for, need not be scathing or offensive. It should reflect the critic's integrity and self-awareness and seek to improve understanding and, ultimately, appreciation for the art form. Chapter 6 deals with negative criticism in detail.

**What's Not Criticism?**

The foregoing characterization of criticism notwithstanding, the boundaries between the activities of the critic, historian, theorist, journalist, etc., are fuzzy at best. Even if one could draw clear, meaningful distinctions between these activities, they would be necessarily tentative and temporal because criticism is one of a number of living disciplines, each with trends and tendencies that influence it. Nevertheless, whether working in a journalistic medium, a scholarly discipline, or as an independent blogger, sharpening your engagement with contemporary culture, knowledge of music, clarity, voice, and values, and consciousness of the boundaries and borders of taste will improve your critical voice.

## Why Do Criticism?

Despite their differences, all critics share the premise that music is something worth investigating and discussing. Is this truism true? After all, isn't the magic of music in that it touches us nonverbally, that it does, in fact, speak for itself? Art critic Dave Hickey condemned his writing as a shadow of the true creative act: "Criticism is the weakest thing you can do in writing. It is the writer's equivalent of air guitar—flurries of silent, sympathetic gestures with nothing at their heart but the memory of the music."[18] Where Hickey deems criticism meaningless, others find it detrimental. A myth persists that the intellectual study of music adulterates its experiential side; that the shift outlined at the beginning of the chapter (from passive listening to active engagement) manifests a shift away from the mysterious pleasures that music provides, toward empty intellectualism. Many have spoken in support of this viewpoint. Experimental jazz legend Ornette Coleman, for instance, seems to confirm this sentiment in the liner notes of his album *Changes of the Century*:

> You can't intellectualize music; to reduce it analytically often is to reduce it to nothing very important. It is only in terms of emotional response that I can judge whether what we are doing is successful or not. If you are touched in some way, then you are in with me.[19]

Certainly, there are many pleasures to be had from musical experience alone, but there are also good reasons for talking about music in a systematic way:

**It seems to be basic to the experience of music in the Western world.**

Thinking and talking about art are basic to the Western human experience. The ancient Greeks did it. The early Christians did it. We are still doing it. Wanting to understand art is, well, understandable. After all, art is often mysterious, and mysteries cry out for clarity. Thinking about how it intersects with society, how it influences behavior, where it fits into our world, is natural. The ancient Greek philosopher, Plato, worried about the powers of music to influence people's thoughts and behaviors. Centuries later, Saint Augustine, a Medieval Christian theologian and philosopher, dedicated a segment of his *Confessions* to the criticism of music, wherein he wrestled with its ambivalent powers—those tending toward a reverence for God and those tending toward gratuitous, sensual pleasure. In the Age of Enlightenment, many thinkers believed the experience of beauty through art and nature opened pathways to one's own inner beauty. Nearly as long as there has been art, there has been the impulse to engage with it critically.

**Not all art gives pleasure primarily to the senses.**

Perhaps some art indeed speaks for itself. Perhaps some music simply enters the ear and creates disinterested pleasure in the listener, like a sunset, but not all music functions in this way. In 1971, Yoko Ono created "Toilet Piece," an unedited recording of a flushing toilet. This is one of a number of ironic anti-art works that proliferated in this period. Its purpose seems to have been to polemicize traditional definitions of art. Its meaning and value cannot be reduced to the sounds themselves. This is conceptual art, and it asks not so much to be heard as to be interrogated.

**Art can mirror life.**

Music tells us something about the times, about our society, and about ourselves. As you will discover over the course of the book, music provides a unique and powerful lens through which to view our changing world. Thus to know music deeply is, in some sense, to know oneself deeply. As such, the journey into criticism is both an outward journey toward music, culture, history, and politics, and an inward journey, toward self-understanding.

## Chapter Summary

What is music criticism? What does it mean to engage with music critically? What distinguishes music criticism from other music discourses? What is the value of music criticism? This chapter introduces these central questions, and in the process touches on central themes of the book. Its key claims are as follows:

- Criticism begins with a shift from the passive consumption to active engagement with music.
- Active engagement defines criticism in the broadest sense.
- Music critics have specific concerns and priorities that distinguish them from other writers on music:
  - Critics are concerned with present-day music culture.
  - Critics operate in the subjective realm of taste.
  - Critics are knowledgeable about music.
  - Some critics operate within systems or schools.

- Critics enhance present-day music culture.
- Taste is a complex philosophical concept that denotes a subjective realm, which is nevertheless distinct from personal preferences and predilections.
- For the eighteenth-century philosopher Immanuel Kant, judgments of taste have two essential elements: subjectivity and (a claim to) universality.
- Criticism can be intertwined with cultural discourses such as Feminism, Queer Theory, Postcolonial Theory, and Capitalist Critique.
- Criticism is culturally and artistically valuable.

## Guide Questions

1. Why is feminism hard to define? What are the central tenets of feminist music criticism?
2. Why can't most of us have a purely aesthetic experience of a cookie?
3. Why did Picasso and others criticize "good taste"?
4. What is the difference between a personal preference and a judgment of taste?
5. Choose a musical example, and write two categories of evaluations, one based on your personal preferences and predilections, and the other based on aesthetic judgment. How do the tone and content change as you move between these two ways of engaging with your song?
6. Using print media and/or the internet, locate one essay in each of the following domains of music: history, journalism, criticism, and fan site. Compare the content and quality of the writing among them. What are the similarities? What are the differences? How does criticism distinguish itself from these other forms of writing?
7. In your opinion, should critics publicly denounce musical works, or should they remain silent on music that they cannot promote?
8. Listen to a song that you enjoy. See if you can move between passive and active engagement with it. What do you experience in each of these states? What are the advantages and disadvantages of each?

## Notes

1 See Arnie Cox, "Embodying Music: The Principles of the Mimetic Hypothesis," *Music Theory: A Journal for the Society of Music Theory* 17, no. 2 (July 2011): 1–24.
2 William Robin, "Beethoven Again," *The New Yorker*, January 17, 2014, accessed February 13, 2017, www.newyorker.com/culture/culture-desk/beethoven-again.
3 "History without footnotes" is the famous subtitle to Chapter eight of mid-century literary critic, Cleanth Brooks's *The Well Wrought Urn: Studies in the Structure of Poetry* (Orlando, FL: Houghton, Mifflin, Harcourt, 1947). For a discussion of the subtitle, see Jerome J. McGann, "The Dawn of the Incommensurate," in *Social Values and Poetic Acts: The Historical Judgment of Literary Work* (Cambridge, MA: Harvard University Press, 1988), 50–72.

4 Laurie Anderson, "Laurie Anderson TALKS Animal Collective's Centipede HZ," *The Talkhouse*, March 7, 2014, accessed March 1, 2017, https://www.talkhouse.com/laurie-anderson-talks-animal-collectives-centipede-hz/.
5 Marc Woodworth and Ally-Jane Grossan, eds., *How to Write About Music* (New York: Bloomsbury, 2015), 63.
6 Immanuel Kant, *Kritik der Urteilskraft*, 1790, §6; trans. as *Critique of the Power of Judgment*, ed. Paul Guyer, trans. Paul Guyer and Eric Matthews (Cambridge: Cambridge University Press, 2000), 97.
7 Immanuel Kant, *Kritik der Urteilskraft*, 1790, §7; trans. as *Critique of the Power of Judgment*, ed. Paul Guyer, trans. Paul Guyer and Eric Matthews (Cambridge: Cambridge University Press, 2000), 98.
8 Cited in Modris Eksteins, *The Rites of Spring: The Great War and the Birth of the Modern Age* (Toronto: Vintage Canada, 2012), 12.
9 Richard Taruskin, "The Musical Mystique: Defending Classical Music against Its Devotees," *The New Republic*, October 22, 2007, accessed March 1, 2017, https://newrepublic.com/article/65641/the-musical-mystique.
10 Edmund Feldman, "The Teacher as Model Critic," *Journal of Aesthetic Education* 7, no. 1 (1973): 50–57.
11 Terry Barrett, *Criticizing Art; Understanding the Contemporary* (Mayfield, 2000), 26.
12 Noël Carroll, *On Criticism* (New York: Routledge, 2009), 93–94.
13 Annamarie Jagose, *Queer Theory: An Introduction* (New York: New York University Press, 1996), 3.
14 Quoted in Jacey Fortin, "Critical Race Theory: A Brief History," *The New York Times*, November 8, 2021, accessed March 15, 2022, www.nytimes.com/article/what-is-critical-race-theory.html.
15 Diarmuid Costello and Jonathon Vickery, eds., *Art: Key Contemporary Thinkers* (New York: Berg, 2007).
16 Rosalind Krauss, quoted by Janet Malcolm, "A Girl of the Zeitgeist—I," *New Yorker*, October 20, 1986, accessed March 1, 2017, www.newyorker.com/magazine/1986/10/20/a-girl-of-the-zeitgeist-I.
17 Carroll, *On Criticism*, 12–14.
18 Dave Hickey, "Air Guitar," in *Air Guitar: Essays on Art and Democracy* (Los Angeles, CA: Art Issues Press, 1997), 163.
19 Cited in David Witzling, *Everybody's America: Thomas Pynchon, Race, and the Cultures of Postmodernism* (New York: Routledge, 2012), 52.

# Part 1
# Aesthetic Foundations

# 1 What Is Art? The Musical Work Problem

A young man sits expectantly in a large concert hall, anticipating a performance of Brahms's first symphony. As the orchestra begins to play, he closes his eyes, savoring those Brahmsian undulations of the slow introduction, which auger a rich musical journey. A novice musician himself, the listener makes note of the counterpoint between the ascending strings and the descending woodwinds, the effect of which is mesmerizing. And yet, has the orchestra not proceeded a tic too quickly to fully exploit that counterpoint? Indeed, it has. At this punchy tempo, the delicate lattice work of interlocking melodies becomes a bit of a jumble. The breathy pauses all but disappear as phrases and ideas collide into one another. As the introduction builds momentum, it registers increasingly as anxious, and the listener becomes steadily more displeased. Turning to his companion at his first opportunity, he remarks, "Brahms' first symphony is unworthy of its place in the canon!"

Is the failure of this performance indeed a failure of Brahms' first symphony? Most of us would agree that it is not. So, what happened in the scenario above? Where did the listener go wrong? To be sure, his observations about the music were incisive. However, he failed to parse out the different domains of music production, assigning praise, criticism, and so forth appropriately among them. In other words, our listener unwittingly conflated the work and the performance. Distinct and differentiated though they are, the line between them is not always so easy to identify. After all, if the music emanating from the orchestra doesn't constitute Brahms' first symphony, what does?

## The Musical Work Concept

This question ushers us into a complex and contested philosophical arena. Consider, by analogy, the world of visual art. Is Figure 1.1 the Mona Lisa? Without question, most of you will answer that it is. Attributed to Leonardo da Vinci and hanging in the Louvre in a gilded frame, the Mona

DOI: 10.4324/9780429505171-3

22  *Aesthetic Foundations*

*Figure 1.1* Leonardo da Vinci, *Mona Lisa (La Giocanda)* 1503

Lisa is one of the most iconic works of art in all of Western history. In fact, the image of the Mona Lisa, reproduced on postcards, napkins, and in art books, is so iconic that it has become in some sense indistinguishable from the original work of art. Now look at Figure 1.2. What is that painting hanging on the wall in that image? Did you once again identify it

*What Is Art? The Musical Work Problem*   23

*Figure 1.2* The *Mona Lisa* in the Louvre, Paris, France 2019
Source: Photo credit, Pedaalemmer

as the Mona Lisa? If so, we have a problem. You have characterized the Mona Lisa as both an iconic, reproducible image and at the same time an indelibly famous and invaluable painting hanging in the Louvre. In the process, you have implicitly acknowledged that the Mona Lisa is both a tangible artifact and a mental image—an object and an idea. In music, this fluidity is even more pronounced because the "artifact" is not an object but rather a sound event, sometimes, but not always, symbolically depicted on a score. Reducible to neither an artifact nor an idea, the musical work must inevitably encompass both. And so we return to the question, *What is Brahms' first symphony?* How does "the work" flow and permeate through a score, a performance, or a recording? If the music that our listener heard was not, in fact, "the work," what is? These questions may seem remote and abstract, but one's implicit answers to them shape the whole project of music criticism.

Consider this 2011 review of Beethoven's Eroica Symphony by Alan Kozinn for *The New York Times*, which negotiates distinctions between the work, its performers, and its performance:

> Alan Gilbert has generally tried to find a balance of elegance and grittiness in his programs with the New York Philharmonic, but it makes sense, now and again, to tip the scale one way or the other. The program Mr. Gilbert conducted on Wednesday evening tilted toward energetic brashness, with Bartok's biting Second Violin Concerto on the first half and Beethoven's "Eroica" Symphony on the second. The orchestra should have had Avery Fisher Hall rocking by the end of the evening, and there were moments when it did. But mostly the performances were more polite than supercharged.
>
> That was particularly the case in the "Eroica," a work larger than life that should deliver a jolt, familiar as it is. Its opening movement, after all, is a huge battle scene, with solid, full orchestra chords standing in for throttling cannon blasts, and a sense of struggle in every bar. In purely technical terms, the execution was close to faultless. Tempos in the outer movements and the Scherzo were brisk, and Mr. Gilbert's account of the Funeral March was plangent, if never quite sublime. The string playing was nimble, focused and warm; the woodwind contributions were consistently shapely; and the brasses had some spectacular moments (especially in the Trio section of the Scherzo).
>
> Missing were the drama and intensity necessary to make the "Eroica" sound fresh and surprising, and to convey a hint of the shock it delivered when it was new. Without that the "Eroica" is merely beloved; it can be much more than that.[1]

This critic moves skillfully between three different ways of engaging with the *Eroica Symphony*. At the outset, he describes the symphony as a work "larger than life," with a "sense of struggle in every bar" of the first movement. Here, he is in essence commending Beethoven himself, and the work is identified as an historically layered construct or idea. Continuing, he remarks that the execution was close to faultless. Tempos, tones and timbres, and development of individual melodic lines were all infallible. In other words, the performance was *technically* well executed, in accordance with the score. Nevertheless, and despite these commendatory remarks, the critic concludes that the performance lacked drama. In the course of this short review, the critic moves nimbly between discussions of the intrinsic composition, technical execution of the performance, and the conductor's interpretation of Beethoven's canonical masterpiece. Beethoven is exalted, the orchestra is commended, and at the same time the conductor, Alan Gilbert, is criticized for his lukewarm engagement with this piece of history. This well-crafted review achieves what our protagonist at the outset of the chapter has not; namely, to distinguish between the work and the given performance of it—a task that begins with identifying the work, itself.

## Getting to Know the Musical Work

In the Western classical music tradition, the work is closely associated with the score. However, whereas in the case of the *Mona Lisa*, the painting constitutes the work, the musical score is simply a symbolic representation of the music, which unfolds in time. In this sense, the score may be thought of as a recipe of sorts. It provides instructions for the creation of the work, and like a recipe, it emphasizes some elements and leaves others unarticulated. Consider this score of the aria from J.S. Bach's 1741 *Goldberg Variations* (ex. 1.1).

This score provides information about the meter (3/4), the key (G Major), and the pitch sequence. For the initiated, the score also provides indications of ornaments (in the little squiggles above certain notes) and an indication of the expressive melodic quality of the piece, represented by the title, *aria*. However, there is no explicit indication of which instrument(s) to use, which ornaments to play, the tempo of the unfolding music, dynamics, mood/affect, or locational aspects of the sound (i.e., sound sources). In 1741, these aspects of the music would have been understood by an interpreter of this score because they were situated within a musical culture. As such, they would have been accommodated by a set of performance practices that dominated a particular genre, style, and historical period.

## Historically Informed Performance (HIP) Movement

Beginning in the 1990s, musicians and conductors have been tasked with honoring these un- (or under-) articulated aspects of music to a greater degree. An entire movement was born, called Historically Informed Performance, or HIP, which argues for attention to performance conventions and technologies that were operative when (and where) a musical work was composed. Originally associated with so-called early music

26  *Aesthetic Foundations*

*Example 1.1* First edition score of the Goldberg Aria, Johann Sebastian Bach, 1741

(music composed before 1750), the HIP movement has generated broad awareness of historical context in classically oriented music performance. HIP performers and scholars are particularly attuned to instruments as a prominent technology that informs musical experience. For example, the modern piano did not exist when J.S. Bach composed the *Goldberg Variations*. They were intended to be performed on a harpsichord. Whereas any number of recordings exist of this work on piano (and more distantly related instruments to the harpsichord), a HIP performance of this piece would use either an antique harpsichord or a modern reconstruction of an authentic historical instrument. (Instrument makers sometimes go so far as to quarry metals and source wood from locations and time periods associated with original instruments.) The timbral characteristics of early instruments can contribute dramatically to the creation of an historically informed sound profile.

HIP performers also source knowledge about musical style. For example, W.A. Mozart was a prolific letter writer, and his thousand-some pages of letters provide invaluable information about musical aesthetics and performance practices in his time. In a letter to his father from October 17, 1777, for example, W.A. Mozart offers numerous insights into the performance practices of eighteenth-century German music:

> Now I'll begin at once with Stein's pianos. Before I had come across any of Stein's make, Späth's claviers had always been my favorites. But now I have to give first place to Stein's because they damp ever so much better than the Regensburg instruments. When I strike hard, I can keep my finger on the note or raise it, but either way, the sound ceases the moment I have produced it. In whatever way I touch the keys, the tone is even. It never jars, it is never stronger or weaker or missing altogether; in a word, it is always even. . . . His instruments have a special advantage over other makes in that they are made with escape action. Only one maker in a hundred bothers about this. But without an escapement you simply can't avoid juddering and shuddering of the hammers after playing the keys. Stein's hammers fall back in an instant once they have struck the strings, whether you hold the keys down or let go of them.[2]

Were you able to discern what might be useful to the historian or HIP performer? For example, Mozart emphasizes the importance of producing an even tone and condemns outdated technologies that employ the hammers in "juddering and shuddering" after sounding the note. These remarks have profoundly shaped our understanding of eighteenth-century keyboard music and Mozart's music in general.

Sometimes, little or no written documentation survives about a performance context. In such cases (and even when written documentation exists), iconography can provide a useful resource for identifying performance practices such as ensemble configurations, modes of holding and playing archaic instruments, performance contexts and locations, symbolic meanings of music and its performance, the social function of music, and even contexts related to socioeconomic status, gender, and race. This 1787 engraving of a flute concert featuring Frederick the Great at his court at Sancoussi provides valuable information about the cultural status and functions of classical music, as well as performance habits and perceptions of court musicians at this time and place. Study this image and try to make some inferences about late eighteenth-century Prussian court music.

We know from this image where different instrumentalists are situated in relation to the keyboard and to each other. We can see that the bass player and cellist are reading from the keyboardist's music rather than from their own. We can observe that the instrumentalists are mostly standing around the harpsichord, and that they are not all facing each other. We see, of course, that there is no conductor. We learn valuable information about body comportment and playing techniques. We see that musicians

*Figure 1.3* Johann Peter Haas's copperplate engraving of *Friedrich II als Flötist bei einem abendlichen Konzert im Jahre 1750*

and audience members are exclusively male, Caucasian, and, judging from the attire, aristocratic. Perhaps you made other observations as well. There is much to learn from images such as this one.

Despite these many resources for reconstructing historical performance practices, until the age of modern recording technology (around 1900), it must be acknowledged that conclusions about historically informed performances are mostly speculative. Furthermore, the catholic adherence to HIP principles can stifle exciting potentialities in these early works. The '70s rock band, Emerson, Lake, and Palmer, recorded a decidedly irreverent version of Mussorgsky's (1874) *Pictures at an Exhibition*, which, though it adheres to none of the HIP principles outlined above, brings Mussorgsky's work into exciting and unique relief; and Glenn Gould's "un-HIP" recordings of J.S. Bach's *Goldberg Variations* on modern piano are some of the best known and most frequently heard recordings of that work. A musical work should therefore be understood as a construct around which recordings, performances, and editions orbit, some in close relation to it and some at greater distance.

### Getting to Know Technical Aspects of the Performance

Beyond knowing the work itself, the critic should know something about how the work should be performed. In other words, the musical work provides a foundation for engaging with technical aspects of a given recording or performance. Critics should familiarize themselves within any extended techniques that a work calls for, as well as being alert to tempo indications, intonation, and the tone and quality of voices and instruments. Vocal music involves diction, pronunciation, and sometimes foreign language articulation. The vocal score (and/or the performance practice associated with a particular piece) can also point to technical features of a performance, through indications of arched phrases, smoothness of line, choral blend, or lyric style, foreign language, rhythmic precision, and intonation.

Sometimes the score itself raises technical issues; some pieces, for example, are published in modern editions with meaningful discrepancies with the original. Consider this edition of the aforementioned Goldberg Aria:

Even if you can't read music, you can perhaps see that there are more notes per measure in Example 1.2 than in Example 1.1. This is because the ornaments are written out in the upper voice of this edition (whereas they were indicated with squiggly lines in the original score), which creates potential gestural differences in the performance of the music, since we can't discern from this edition which notes are primary and which are ornamental. (To put it another way, ornaments should be experienced as parenthetical, and Example 1.2 presents them without parentheses.) Furthermore, tied notes in the original are not always transmitted as ties in this edition, and accidentals are altered, such that even the pitches themselves are here and there different in the two versions. In response to discrepancies such as these, critical and urtext editions have become standard in recent decades, particularly among HIP performers and scholars, and some performers prefer to read from facsimile editions, which duplicate exactly the original manuscript of a work.

## Getting to Know Interpretive Aspects of the Performance

In some ways, interpretive aspects of a performance are harder to pin down than technical ones. When Allan Kozinn criticized Gilbert's performance of Beethoven's Third Symphony as lacking drama, he ushered the reader into the realm of expression. For Gilbert, Beethoven's *Eroica* Symphony should feel larger than life; it should "wow" the listener. There is no question that music acts on us emotionally. Philosophers and scholars of music have theorized since antiquity about this unquestionable—and unquestionably mysterious—aspect of musical experience. Over the course of this book we will engage with this aspect of criticism in more detail. At present it suffices to raise these questions about a given performance: *What is the affect or emotional tenor of the piece being performed? What was left unsaid in the score (and therefore left to interpretation)? What liberties were taken with the music in this*

*Example 1.2* Aria from the Goldberg Variations, Johann Sebastian Bach, 1741, Arranged and Edited by RSB, 2011.

*particular interpretation?* A good place to begin to explore musical interpretation is to listen to multiple versions of a given musical work, noting similarities and differences between them.

### The Musical Work and Value

Any discussion of the musical work should conclude with a discussion of the canon, musical value, and music history because these concerns underlie all engagements with the musical work. We can probably agree that when I sit down to improvise at the piano, I am not producing a musical work, skillful though I may be. We may also agree that "Happy Birthday" is not a musical work and that Beethoven's ninth symphony is. But why? This is because the musical work is not merely an (any) artifact of musical production. In order to qualify as (Capital-W) Work, some scholars argue that a piece of music must be (1) discrete, (2) attributable, and (3) reproducible:[3]

## Discrete

Undifferentiated noise does not generally qualify as a musical work. A piece of music must begin, end, and distinguish itself from the surrounding soundscape of nature or other music or what have you. In other words, a musical work is discrete and differentiated.

## Attributable

It is also attributable in that it points back to an author or creator. "Happy Birthday" is most certainly discrete, but it is not attributable, and it therefore does not project values of a particular time, place, and creative voice.

## Reproducible

Thirdly, according to this system, a musical work can be reproduced or recreated. It must stand apart from any individual performance of it. If a given performance cannot be reproduced, it cannot be distinguished from its soundscape. A jazz improvisation may indeed be discrete and attributable, but (unless it is recorded), it is generally not considered to be reproducible; it is rather identified with a specific performative moment and is therefore not in itself a musical work.

Is it stable? Is it reproducible? Is it attributable? These questions, though they are essential to a critic's engagement with a musical experience, should not be confused with questions of value. Much musical activity operates outside of the narrow construct of the musical work, and the critic must have alternative tools in order to engage effectively with them. The fragility of the musical work concept becomes particularly apparent in considering popular music.

## The Case of Popular Music

In contemporary mainstream popular music, "the work" (though it's rarely labeled as such) is not typically associated with a score. The work is more often located in an alternative artifact, the recording; a performance is an interpretation of that recording (and/or vice versa), and the whole project of classical music criticism is flipped on its side. Nevertheless, an engagement with popular music demands many of the same skills and knowledge as with classical music.

Consider the following example: On August 28, 2013 Paul McCartney released the single (and title track of the upcoming album), *New*, to the iTunes store and Sound Cloud. Seventy-one-year old McCartney croons over a boisterous band that chugs along with a clap-track back beat, harpsichord, and punctuating horn blasts: "You came along and made my life a song; one lucky day you came along, just in time. Well I was searching for a rock. You came along, and then we were new." A little time capsule of 1960s rock "n" roll, the song is undeniably charming. But new? Not so much.

The contradiction between the evident nostalgia of the track's sound profile and the title asks to be puzzled out. Doing so inevitably pulls us out of the song itself to consider the sound world of The Beatles and 1960s rock "n" roll in general, the trajectory of Paul McCartney's solo career—indeed, his last original album was called *Memory Almost Full*—and the cyclical nature of popular music culture more broadly. Whether *New* should be heard as an out of touch grasping of a once-genius septuagenarian musician, or an ironic excursion into the fragile romance of nostalgia, is an open question. Regardless, to engage with this song and this album is to necessarily engage with its context. Consider the following review by Kevin E.G. Perry. The review begins by placing McCartney among other rock legends who have remained relevant or returned to the spotlight.

> Perhaps it's a symptom of our nostalgia-obsessed age, but over the last decade or so rock'n'roll has shed the stigma of getting older.[4] Quips have been made about The Rolling Stones' advancing decrepitude since they were lithe fiftysomethings, yet this summer, on the cusp of their seventies, they became the most popular headliners in Glastonbury history. Ten years ago, new David Bowie albums were met with mild dread and disinterest; today, they are bona fide cultural events. The same applies to Bob Dylan, who's currently enjoying the kind of acclaim he has not known since the 1970s; and Fleetwood Mac, whose last few reunion tours weren't quite the hipster circle-jerks the latest one has inexplicably become. Put simply, there's never been a better time to be a pensionable rock legend with a new record.

Next, he situates *New* within McCartney's output, observing that the album indeed seems to be striving for something current:

> All of which augurs well for Paul McCartney's first collection of new songs in six years. His last album, "Kisses On The Bottom"—2012's

well-intentioned but utterly extraneous set of pre-Elvis jazz standards—couldn't have sounded more septuagenarian if it had been given away with The Mail On Sunday. By contrast, "New" initially seems in danger of veering too far in the opposite direction: there's that godawful name for starters, not to mention the presence of It-producers such as Mark Ronson and Paul Epworth, two guys who fit the profile of what you imagine McCartney considers "with it". Happily, "New" avoids becoming another thumbs-akimbo entry into the Groovy Uncle Paul canon; instead, it's his most enjoyable record in years.

At this point, the author engages with the music, locating the title track, "New," in McCartney's Beatles-era sound world:

> The title track is probably the best example of this. "New" sounds like the work of a younger McCartney—47 years younger, if the "Revolver"-ish brass arrangement and melodic cap-doff to 'Got To Get You Into My Life' are anything to go by—and Ronson's retro-modernist production talents, far from sounding gimmicky, serve the song well. Indeed, it's a shame that he only worked on two of the 13 tracks (there's a "hidden" track called 'Scared'), particularly when the other one—the psychedelic whirligig of "Alligator"—is better still. Likewise, you'll hear echoes of "Blackbird" on 'Early Days', although that song's sentimental look back to the beginning of The Beatles is marred by McCartney's longstanding preoccupation with ensuring everyone knows he was John Lennon's equal, and not his junior partner. "Everybody seems to have their own opinion of who did this and who did that", he grumbles, before asserting "they can't take it from me".

Following are remarks on the album's less successful moments (including the choice of title):

> By now you've probably guessed that the album's title is something of a misnomer, and that much of "New" sounds quite familiar. But the track in which McCartney takes the title literally is one of the album's few misfires. "Appreciate", with its synthetic R&B drums and light-industrial guitars, is the sort of thing everyone involved probably congratulated themselves for, but it sits awkwardly with the rest of the songs.
> 
> There are a few others that don't quite work—"Looking At Her" tries to enliven a rote and unremarkable melody by punctuating it with strangled synth ululations, while "Hosanna" is every bit as predictable as its title would suggest—and it goes without saying that any homage to the past never comes anywhere close to bettering it.

Concluding, the author assures us that there is nothing new about *New*:

> Still, if anyone has earned the right to stop being judged by his own superhuman body of work, surely it's Paul McCartney. Don't be misled by the title: "New" is the sound of an old dog having fun with some old tricks.

For this critic, both what works and what doesn't are rooted in the musical universe surrounding the album. This critique steps outside of the pure sound profile to consider McCartney's artistic career, influences, and allusions in the album, McCartney's personal biography, and the album's label and producers. To be sure, there is a time or place for engaging with pure sound; the rhythmic profile of McCartney's melody flits about in the verse until it takes flight in the chorus, soaring with the long breathed notes. His reedy, 71-year old voice carries nicely in the falsetto range. And the harpsichord adds a nice touch of whimsy and just the slightest earthy twang to balance out all of that syrupy sweetness. Indeed, much can be said about the sound world alone, but the critic goes beyond even the most delightful and vivid descriptions.

The success of this essay is predicated on the critic's knowledge of the context of this album and his ability to situate this review within it. Just as with the classical musical work, discussed above, the meaning and value of this song are networked to history and history in the making. In other words, the success of this review is predicated on the critic's knowledge of the context of this album and his ability to situate this interpretation within it.

### The Artist

Who is the artist? How does this song or album relate to the rest of their canon? Is this a departure from the artist's earlier work? How does this music (and does this music) reflect the personal history of the artist? In the case of McCartney, the artist is (as I write this) a 71-year old megastar whose ten years as a Beatle shaped the entire landscape of rock 'n' roll. We learn that *New* is the septuagenarian's 24th studio album, and the album title—both understated with a mere nine straight lines depicting the word and overstated with those lines lit in pink neon—is thus a decisive point of interest. After all, the title track, from its first unfolding, assures us that we will be enjoying McCartney of old. *New* isn't about new sounds or new directions in music. It is about McCartney's renewal. Tracing his artistic history back provides further context for this argument. His 23rd album, we read, was one of solipsistic melancholy, and from this perspective, *New* is reinforced as an emotional, rather than artistic renewal.

## The Album

Getting to know an album begins with listening. The critic of the Paul McCartney album seems to have listened with these essential questions in mind: Does the album have an internal logic; a narrative or concept that pulls the individual tracks together? Which songs work well together? Which songs seem out of place? How does the track under review relate to the album as a whole? How does the album relate to other albums in the genre? How does the album sit with the rest of the band's output? One should also consider who produced the album and on what label. Production can be so essential to an album's sound—especially in contemporary, technology-based music—that fans now follow producers like they once did artists. Consider, for example, the album *True Colors*, produced by the Russian-German phenom, Zedd. The album features collaborations with big-name stars, and yet the cover presents Zedd as the artist/creator.

*Figure 1.4* Album Cover for Zedd, *True Colors*, 2015

36  Aesthetic Foundations

*Intertextual Networks*

Professional critics challenge themselves to identify resonances with the artist or band's earlier work and with other bands in the genre. There is no shortcut to this kind of literacy, but you will have more authority when examining music that you know really well. If you are an exclusive hip-hop listener, you might have a hard time talking meaningfully about Brad Paisley. If you only listen to '70s rock, you might not have much to say about EDM. Start with what you know and work to expand your musical universe over time.

Think of your favorite song on your favorite album by your favorite band in your favorite genre. If you imagine writing that name in the center of a piece of paper, you could start to draw connections outward toward other bands, other works that the band has produced, life experiences of band members, and cultural and historical events that influenced the band. The professional critic has a grasp of many such musical universes as well as the connections among them. Of course, not all is lost if you do not have total bibliographic control of the genre at hand. Did you hear the pungent clanging of the harpsichord on "New"? A quick internet search of popular songs with harpsichord provides a starting point for making comparisons. This slow and steady work gradually grows into professional music literacy.

**Chapter Summary**

This chapter teaches emerging critics to navigate the philosophical problem of the music work. If I show you an image of the *Mona Lisa* and ask you what it is, you may indeed say that it's the *Mona Lisa*, when in fact the *Mona Lisa* is hanging in the *Louvre*. This raises a philosophical distinction between art as a physical object and art as the image projected by the object. With music the distinction is even more complex. Whereas a work of visual art encompasses both the image and the object itself, the concept of a musical work can move between the score, a given performance, an (imaginary) ideal performance, and a recording. Because of this fluidity, the critic must be aware at any given moment of what they are critiquing: intrinsic aspects of the composition, technical aspects of a performance or production, or interpretive aspects of a given realization of the work. The main points of the chapter are as follows:

- A musical work is a complex philosophical concept.
- The notion of work can move between the score, a given performance, an imagined or ideal performance, and a recording.
- Different notions of the work give rise to different critical lenses.
- A critic of music may focus on
  - Intrinsic aspects of a composition
  - Technical aspects of a performance

- Interpretive aspects of a performance
- Classical music culture tends to privilege the score and places value on the performer's ability to realize the perceived intentions of the composer.
- Popular music culture tends to privilege live experiences, performativity, and immediacy. The score in popular music is often descriptive and secondary.

## Guide Questions

1. What are some differences between HIP performances and non-HIP performances of classical music?
2. Why is the HIP movement not usually relevant in popular music?
3. What are the key dimensions of a musical work that a critic must differentiate in a review?
4. What are some of the ways that historians and critics determine how music of the (distant) past sounded?
5. Should we strive to recreate music of the past as it originally sounded? Why or why not?
6. What are the considerations in popular music that determine a work's meaning and value?

## Notes

1 Allan Kozinn, "Renderings Energetic and Brash," *New York Times*, May 5, 2011, accessed June 2, 2020, https://www.nytimes.com/2011/05/06/arts/music/new-york-philharmonic-plays-bartok-and-beethoven-review.html.
2 October 17, 1777: "Nun muß ich gleich bey die steinischen Piano forte anfangen. Ehe ich noch vom stein seiner arbeit etwas gesehen habe, waren mir die spättischen Clavier die liebsten; Nun muß ich aber den steinischen den vorzug lassen; denn sie dämpfen noch viell besser, als die Regensburger. wenn ich starck anschlage, ich mag den finger liegen lassen, oder aufheben, so ist halt der ton in dem augenblick vorbey, da ich ihn hören ließ. ich mag an die Claves kommen wie ich will, so wird der ton immer gleich seyn. er wird nicht schebern, er wird nicht stärcker, nicht schwächer gehen, oder gar ausbleiben; mit einem wort, es ist alles gleich . . . seine instrumente haben besonders das vor andern eigen, daß sie mit auslösung gemacht sind. da giebt sich der hunderteste nicht damit ab. aber ohne auslösung ist es halt nicht möglich daß ein Piano forte nicht schebere oder nachklinge; seine hämmerl, wen man die Claves anspielt, fallen, in dem augenblick da sie an die saiten hinauf springen, wieder herab, man mag den Claves liegen lassen ode auslassen." Bauer and Deutsch, eds., *Briefe und Aufzeichnungen*, 2: 68; trans., Anderson, *Letters*, 327–328.
3 Michael Talbot, ed., *The Musical Work: Reality or Invention?* (Liverpool: Liverpool University Press, 2017), 3.
4 Kevin E. G. Perry, "Paul McCartney—'New'," October 14, 2013, accessed July 15, 2019, https://www.nme.com/reviews/reviews-paul-mccartney-14852-320542.

## 2   Music and Authenticity

In the world of classical music, the composer and performer are often distinct and differentiated. For this reason, the meeting of a glorious piece of music and a gifted performer warrants special attention. Such is the case (or so it would seem) with the Gounod/Bach "Ave Maria," which is hailed as one of the great artifacts of classical music. (Charles Gounod composed the piece by superimposing the Latin Ave Maria prayer over a minimally altered version of the J.S. Bach's Prelude No. 1 in C Major.) When it was recorded by Alessandro Moreschi of the Sistine Chapel Choir, the piece was further elevated to achieve an "unearthly" quality.[1] Reviewers found Moreschi's 1904 recording of this piece "beautiful, ethereal, and a little bit disturbing."[2] Reading about Moreschi's famous "Ave Maria," you are warned that it "will haunt you forever; the purity, power, range."[3]

Such commendations of Moreschi's recording are numerous, as review upon review promises that the piece will be "unlike anything you have ever heard."[4] Yet, listening to Moreschi's "Ave Maria" recording, one might be hard-pressed to find the magic so frequently heard by critics. Even behind the distracting crackles and pops of the crude recording technology, and dismissing the heavy touch on the piano, Moreschi's voice sounds a bit thin, unsteady, one might even say, amateurish. So, what do these critics know that we do not? The answer is that Alessandro Moreschi was, at the time of this recording, believed to be the last living castrato and the only one to survive the age of reliable recording technology.

The term *castrato* refers to a classical male singer who has undergone castration before reaching puberty in order to preserve his prepubescent vocal range. Castration prevented the boy's larynx from being transformed by the physiological changes of puberty. His prepubescent vocal range (similar to that of a female) was therefore largely preserved, while other inevitable physiological changes distinguished his voice from that of a child's. Due to a lack of testosterone, the castrato's bone joints did not harden in the usual manner; thus, the bones of his limbs and ribs grew unusually long. The resultant expanded chest cavity (in combination with

DOI: 10.4324/9780429505171-4

intensive vocal training) gave the castrato extraordinary lung and breath capacity. Neither entirely representative of a biological male or female, adult or child, the *idea* of the castrato is, for some, indeed "unearthly" and, given the conditions of the surgeries and age of patients (as young as seven), more than "a little bit disturbing."

The earliest castrati were employed by the Catholic Church in sixteenth-century Rome, where women were not permitted to sing professionally, but where soprano voice parts were denoted in scores. By the eighteenth century, castrati dominated both the theater and church (despite that the practice of castration was officially illegal). The custom fell out of public favor over the course of the nineteenth century, and by the millennium—and the advent of modern recording technology—only one castrato was known to have survived, Alessandro Moreschi.

Did critics indeed find Moreschi's voice hauntingly beautiful? Perhaps, but it is almost certain that they found his story to be so. Tragic and romantic to the extreme, the castrato reinforces our most enduring mythologies of the suffering artist. Moreover, and perhaps more importantly, Moreschi provides a last fragile wedge in the door to an evocative, if sometimes macabre, historical practice. Akin to the historically informed performance practice movement, which promotes attention to the instruments, conditions, and performance practices of a musical work at its time and place of creation, Moreschi calls attention to unique and inimitable aspects of music history as well as our concern with experiencing them authentically.

## Defining Authenticity

And so we enter a notoriously slippery realm of aesthetics, in which people, relationships, stories, commercials, products, and to be sure, musical works and artists, are evaluated by means of the nebulous credentials of authenticity. Nebulous, indeed. For although few would dispute Moreschi's authenticity, his particular credentials—childhood surgical mutilation combined with intense vocal training—are by no means transferable to musicians at large. Alessandro Moreschi, Kendrick Lamar, and Billie Holiday have all been hailed as authentic musicians, and yet the authenticating strategies of these artists could not be more disparate. Fittingly, the Oxford English Dictionary observes at least seven meanings of the word "authenticity":[5]

(a) *The fact or quality of being true or in accordance with fact, veracity, and correctness.*
(b) *The fact or quality of being authoritative or duly authorized.*
(c) *The fact or quality of being authentic, genuineness.*
(d) *The quality of truthful correspondence between inner feelings and their outward expression; unaffectedness, sincerity.*

*(e) The quality or fact of accurately reflecting a model or exemplar, or of being traditionally produced or presented.*
*(f) A mode of existence arising from self-awareness, critical reflection on one's goals and values, and responsibility for one's own actions; the condition of being true to oneself.*
*(g) The fact or quality of being real; actuality, reality.*

These definitions highlight the complexities of any attribution of this word. Consider, for example, the implicit tensions between definitions *e* and *f*. *E, The quality or fact of accurately reflecting a model or exemplar*, is predicated on imitation, modeling, and tradition and is in this sense external; *f, the condition of being true to oneself*, is by contrast inward looking, as it focuses on knowing and honoring one's unique inner self. In light of these two definitions, a person or object can be authentic in one sense while violating the dictates of authenticity in yet another. Thus we are met with our first, and perhaps most frustrating, tenet of authenticity in music:

**There are no attributes of musical artists or works that are universally designated authentic.**

Authenticity indeed means different things in different cultural and historical contexts. And yet, there is no question that authenticity is a significant measure of value; in this way, music mirrors the broader public sphere. The world of advertising provides ample evidence of the premium placed on authenticity. Consider, for example, a recent campaign for Victorinox Swiss Army watches, whose tagline claims to "turn the 'fashion ad featuring famous celebrity' on its head," focusing instead on "welders, photographers, and firefighters—the *true* appreciators of a finely crafted watch—to stand by the hardworking nature of a Victorinox Swiss Army timepiece." The campaign is referred to as "Inspired by Authenticity," exhibiting the reach of this concept in the commercial world.[6]

Here, as with Moreschi, cultural values are transferred and projected onto the artifact under consideration. Thus the timepiece is deemed "hardworking" (like the welders and firefighters that would wear it) and the "Ave Maria," haunting (like the history itself). Of course, we can't know for certain how critics would have responded to Moreschi's recording were it not such a compelling historical artifact; however, we can be certain that its authenticity adds much to our experience of the piece. This recasting of authenticating attributes as aesthetic qualities is a common feature of music criticism and comprises the second of five central tenets of authenticity:

**Authenticity is not in itself an aesthetic category, but it shapes our aesthetic responses and evaluations.**

As such the designation "authentic" often seems to indicate accordance with some agreed-upon criteria that situates it in a group which conforms to a model. Membership in an authenticating group or proximity to the original culture of that group provides the substance of a particular artist's authenticating credentials. Moreschi's group—living castrati—highlights his unique status and thus substantiates his authenticity. It thus follows that the determination of authenticity begins with identifying the original culture—the worldview, beliefs, customs, history, shared experiences, language, and/or everyday life of a coherent group of people—and its expression in music. In what follows, we will take, by example, the American folk music revival.

## Folk Authenticity

Music has long been a source of group identification, articulating and delineating characteristics of nation, race, ethnicity, gender, socioeconomic status, sexuality and other aspects of identity. Folk music in particular highlights aspects of a collective self. Although the term *folk* can mean a variety of things, historians and scholars generally agree that folk culture (like folk music) operates in distinction to mass culture, elite culture, urban culture, and the professional or academic sphere. The term itself, related to German *Volk*, meaning "the people," signals that folk denotes the voice of a group rather than an individual. Historically, folk music was transmitted orally, through informal social structures, such as family, friends, and work-life, rather than formal institutions, such as churches and courts. Folk music is also traditionally participatory rather than presentational and performance-oriented. It is often associated with rural culture and with lower socioeconomic classes. Finally, being participatory, orally transmitted, and non-presentational, folk music is often considered amateur music and therefore, again, music of and for the people.

As an emblem and voice of rural, working class society, folk music in the United States was increasingly politicized over the course of the twentieth century in its opposition to corporate capitalism and mass culture. The American folk music revival reached a national platform in the 1950s and '60s and merged with liberal antiwar and civil rights activism in figures, such as Bob Dylan, The Weavers, and Peter, Paul, and Mary. Bob Dylan, in particular, captures the tensions surrounding authenticity in the folk movement and their expressions in sound. His "Times They Are A-Changin'" exhibits the characteristic elements of the American folk music revival and their politicization in music.

One quick listen to this song brings Dylan's grainy, anti-classical voice into relief. There is no apparent effort to smooth over the natural grain in his voice, which carries forth without any pretense. Unpolished and unprofessional, the music is presented not as an end in itself but rather a vehicle for the transmission of Dylan's poetic musings.

The second feature of this song that merits attention is the phrasing. Phrasing concerns the syntax of lyrics or poetry. Consider the first stanza of Shakespeare's Sonnet Five (1609). Each line contains ten syllables, and, as such, the poem unfolds with a lilting, regular rhythm:

> Those hours, that with gentle work did frame
> The lovely gaze where every eye doth dwell,
> Will play the tyrants to the very same
> And that unfair which fairly doth excel:

We could disturb this symmetry by simply changing the syllable count:

> Those hours, that with work did frame
> The loveliest gaze where every single eye doth dwell,
> Play tyrants to the same
> And that unfair which fairly doth excel

Just as the poem flows more naturally when the accents, syllable counts, and rhyme schemes unfold regularly and predictably, a popular song will generally satisfy the ears more readily if its phrases are regular and predictable in length. In the case of Dylan, however, no such regularity is intended. Rather, Dylan comes in—unpredictably—in the middle of the third measure, and the subsequent musical phrases have unequal lengths that are marked by the incongruous relationship between the music and poetry: five measures, four measures, six measures, four measures, and so on. While irregular phrasing can in some instances be a measure of complexity in music, in this case, it seems to point to an unregulated, improvisatory compositional process, suggesting that the poetry flows freely and unconfined from the mind and heart of the singer.

Finally, and perhaps most emblematically, the song features only simple, portable instruments. There are no electric or amplified instruments, nor even stationary acoustic ones (like a drum kit or a piano) on this track. Portable, acoustic instruments are hallmarks of the folk aesthetic, as they turn us away from large, mediated venues; as such, acoustic instruments not only represent intimacy—unlike highly processed technology-based sounds—they also police it by ensuring that audiences remain small and settings intimate.

One envisions Dylan as a modern-day troubadour, ambling through towns and cities with only his guitar and harpsichord for company. Although his 1966 song, "Mr. Tambourine Man" does feature minimal electric guitar, there are no drums or bass, and it features the characteristic elements of folk music described above, including verses of varying lengths, irregular phrasing, and a dreamy poetic text. And yet there seems to have been something about this song that pointed to the commercial mainstream; at least, that seems to be how The Byrds heard it. The West Coast sixties rock band reconceived "Mr. Tambourine Man" for a mainstream mass audience, which it penetrated and dominated, reaching number one on both US and UK charts. (Dylan never achieved a number one hit.) The Byrds' cover of "Tambourine Man" reveals fundamental changes to the song's instrumentation, form and meter, length, and affect, as outlined below:

*Instrumentation*

A mainstream rock song should have backing drums and electric guitar, which can be heard on The Byrds cover.

*Structure*

A four-piece rock band with backing drums demands a regular, coordinated structure. Furthermore, popular music for mass consumption should appeal primarily to the body with a discernible, danceable beat. Therefore, the phrase structure and meter must be regulated, as they are in The Byrds' version.

*Length*

Popular songs in this period catered to record formats and radio play. Therefore, such songs should be short and catchy. The Byrds preserved only two verses of Dylan's "Mr. Tambourine Man" and left the rest of the lengthy song out.

*Affect*

The sincere, poetic folk song by Dylan is, in the hands of The Byrds, reimagined as an expression of 1960s psychedelia.

While Dylan's version remained a marginal folk song, The Byrds' cover dominated in both the US and the UK charts. This exhibits a tension that runs through popular music culture between the dictates of authenticity and those of the commercial marketplace. Here is evidence of our third principle of authenticity:

> Mass culture, pop culture, consumer culture, and celebrity culture are almost always foils for authentic expression, which is rooted in community and/or individual experience.

Dylan is thus the emblem of the true, genuine artist, which leads us from the realm of the aesthetic to that of the moral. To be authentic is to be in some sense honest, and as such, claims of authenticity are almost always positive. Returning to the Victorinox advertisement, this aspect of authenticity is fully exploited in the campaign. *Truth. Hard Work. Honor.* These words sketch the image of the authentic consumer of the Victorinox timepiece as a good, honest American. Furthermore, by critiquing the mainstream "fashion ad featuring famous celebrity," Victorinox distances its brand from one of the most notoriously inauthentic sectors: mass culture. In music, too, that produced for a mass consumer market is frequently deemed derivative and inauthentic.

If musical authenticity seems to be coming into focus, at least within a particular genre, it is nevertheless complicated by time. Consider, for example, Joseph O'Connell's 2018 release, *Genericana*. Like Dylan, O'Connell, who uses the stage name, Elephant Micah, presents himself as a folk musician; however, his music—as revealed on the first hearing—is far removed from that of his predecessor. As this suggests,

**The dictates of authenticity, even within a culture or genre, change over time.**

*Genericana* certainly does not project a Dylan-esque folk authenticity. Nevertheless, critics consistently locate the album's authenticity and appeal within the tropes and tenets of folk culture. For Brian Howe, writing for *Pitchfork, for example,*

> The change in Elephant Micah's music feels at least partly related to a change in scenery. A former resident of Indiana, where he worked as a folklorist, O'Connell now lives in North Carolina, a couple of hours from the coast. If his old music had something familiar, landlocked, and level about it, *Genericana* is shaped by both the stranger's fresh perspective on new terrain and the ambient call of the sea.[7]

O'Connell is authorized as a once folklorist, and his new sound profile is positioned as geographically or locationally grounded: we are invited to relate the landscape of Indiana to his earlier sound and the romantic call of the sea to this new one.

Furthermore, the music, we are told, doesn't seek to surprise but rather to beguile; it doesn't aim for grandeur. It is, instead, a slow, philosophical burn of a listening experience, grounded always in nature. For Allan Jones, writing for *Uncut,*

> The first thing you hear, on a track called "Surf A", sounds like the sea, where everything comes from our watery genesis. Waves appear to crash on a beach somewhere. Seagulls squawk in circling overhead flight. It's like a field recording from the beginning of time, or thereabouts. But the noise you're listening to is made by a homemade synthesiser called The

Mutant, a contraption likely built by a boffin with electrified hair and an obsession with obsolete technologies.[8]

Even the discussions of the synthetic elements on the album, like the one above, read like a list of credentials for a discussion of folk authenticity: the synth itself is DIY, analog, and stamped (if only metaphorically and by association) with the *Moog* label, the name in older generation analog synthesizers. As Robin Smith observes, "alongside his acoustic fumblings and brushed drum strokes, O'Connell utilises tape decks and oscillating synths, creating a kind of naturalistic ambiance in which his folk music can languish."[9] Sarah Lay notes even more pointedly that "from 'devalued or discarded' gear, the record twists the sound of Americana as it finds new ways of interacting with instruments."[10] Time and again, critics privilege these technological anachronisms for their perceived authenticity. *Genericana's* reviewers exhibit evident nostalgia for the past, highlight connections to nature, and celebrate his unmediated, DIY sensibility. And so, underneath more contemporary accommodations for technology, urban spaces, the popular marketplace, etc., is an allegiance to those broader tenets that governed folk authenticity in the creative hands of Bob Dylan.

## Authenticity in Hip-Hop

Truth, genuineness, sincerity, turning away from the marketplace, rejection of mass culture; these values separate Bob Dylan and Elephant Micah from The Byrds and Katy Perry. However, they only go so far to elucidate authenticity in hip-hop. There is no question that authenticity is an essential feature of all hip-hop artistry and criticism; however, it may express itself in ways that are specific to the culture, politics, and history of the art form. Kembrew McLeod is among those scholars to have advanced a theory of authenticity in hip-hop. He outlines six major domains of authenticity in the genre: social-psychological, racial, political-economic, gender-sexual, social-locational, and cultural. Authenticity in each of these domains is contrasted with inauthenticity as outlined in the table below:[11]

McLeod's system provides an excellent starting point for a consideration of authenticity in hip-hop. One can readily see how iconic nineties rappers like Ice Cube and Public Enemy articulate the tenets of realness, hardness, urban-ness, blackness, etc., in their music and personae. However, in considering hip-hop authenticity in general and McLeod's system in specific, one must confront several important caveats:

### Storytelling

There's no question that hip-hop exalts the tenet of "keepin' it real"; Spice 1 was quoted in the nineties as saying, "Basically, I'mma try to make my art the same thing as my life. In the past, my life was going where my art was

## 46  Aesthetic Foundations

*Table 2.1* "Support Claims of Authenticity," From Kembrew McLeod, "Authenticity within Hip Hop and Other Cultures Threatened with Assimilation," 139.

| Domain | Authentic | Inauthentic |
| --- | --- | --- |
| Social-psychological | Speaking the truth, keeping it real in lyrics, reflecting the artist's lived experience | Lyrics that don't reflect the artist's lived experience |
| Racial | POC | White |
| Political-Economic | Underground, DIY | Mainstream, commercial |
| Gender-Sexual | Stereotypically masculine, machismo, and heterosexual | Feminine, queer, |
| Social-Locational | Urban, inner city, hood | Suburban |
| Cultural | Connects to hip-hop's original cultural and expressions in graffiti, DJing, breakdancing, and rapping | No connection to hip-hop's original culture |

going because I try to keep it as real as I can."[12] Nevertheless, some contemporary hip-hop seems to turn on a different approach to authenticity than the "art mirrors life" one. In such cases, lyrics are not so much chronicles of lived experience as interpretive stories that play off of the inner world of the artist. Consider Kendrick Lamar: time and again, critics interweave themes of storytelling, lived experience, and hyperbole in their analyses of Lamar's music. For Lisa Robinson, writing for *Vanity Fair*, Lamar is cast as "the poet laureate of hip-hop, perceptive, philosophical, unapologetic, fearless, and an innovative storyteller whose body of work has been compared to James Joyce and James Baldwin."[13] For Matthew Trammell, similarly, "storytelling has been Lamar's greatest skill and most primary mission, to put into (lots of) words what it's like to grow up as he did—to articulate, in human terms, the intimate specifics of daily self-defense from your surroundings."[14] Referring to "Duckworth," however, Trammel goes further to remark that the story is "delivered with such precision, vivid detail, and masterful pacing that it can't possibly be true. But it's a tale too strange to be fiction, and too powerful not to believe in—just like its author."[15]

### Hyperreality

Trammell's remarks about the inscrutable line between fact and fiction points to the postmodern concept of the hyperreal. The hyperreal is an aesthetic category that operates on the boundary between what we accept as real and what we know to be false. Consider this 2007 photograph by Filip DuJardin:

The above image is one of a series of hyperreal (and photoshopped) images called *Fictions*. This image resides on the border between the real and the imaginary, thus effacing the boundary between them. The image

Music and Authenticity  47

*Figure 2.1* Filip Dujardin, *Fictions*, 2007

itself is photographic, meticulous, and accurate, but the content is extreme, bizarre, and, for some, perhaps even unsettling. (Would you want the corner office on the overhang?) Hyperreality is a performed ironic reality that exhibits how untrustworthy our own perceptions can be. The hyperreal is a prominent artistic strategy in hip-hop, as seen in sounds of gun shots, whining helicopter blades, and in presumed real-life controversies and beefs among rappers. Lamar's album *DAMN.* provides a vivid example of the hyperreal by presenting as a palindrome, opening and closing with gunshots and a reference to talking a walk. In an interview with *MTV News*, Lamar explains:

> The initial vibe listening from the top all the way to the bottom is . . . this aggression and this attitude. You know, "DNA," and exposing who I really am. You listen from the back end, and it's almost the duality and the contrast of the intricate Kendrick Lamar. Both of these pieces are who I am.[16]

For the listener, the palindromic nature of the album unsettles its prominent narrative trajectory, complicating its meaning and undermining any easy assurances about Lamar's message. On the other hand, the fact that the album coheres in both directions, conveying two stories that are as true as they are different, seems to reinforce the realism of the stories it contains. It is in this paradox that we find evidence of the hyperreal.

*Globalization*

Hip-hop is, and will always be, rooted in the experience of post-Civil Rights era urban Black America. This is not to say that Caucasian rappers are inherently inauthentic, but a white rapper like Eminem must—and indeed did—address their outsider status in order to remain relevant. (Mickey Hess employs the term "inversion" to describe Eminem's enunciation of his whiteness.[17] For Hess, Eminem, who presented his whiteness as a hindrance to his acceptance as a rapper,[18] thus framed himself a racial outsider both different from and yet analogous to hip-hop's core demographic.) For Kendrick Lamar, by contrast, racial authenticity is uncontested and skillfully harnessed: For Marcus J. Moore, in his book *The Butterfly Effect: How Kendrick Lamar Ignited the Soul of Black America*, the author aligns Lamar with other black musicians who "created music in which we could see our full, beautiful selves . . . and helped us remember that we weren't second-class citizens, even when the world tried to render us invisible."[19]

In *DAMN.*, critics hear an expansion of the black consciousness of his previous work that transcends the traditional black-white binary: "If he was 'black as the moon' on his last album, he's an 'Israelite' here, refusing to identify himself by the shade of his skin but fluent in the contents of his DNA."[20] For another critic, similarly, Black Israelism is, for Kendrick, a type of religious bricolage that "communicates black chosen-ness" and thus expands, without relinquishing, his racial identity and authenticity.[21] The roots of hip-hop in the genre-pioneers' resistance to systemic racism of post-Civil-Rights era black and brown America remain strong and provide artists like Lamar the opportunity to articulate a self that both honors and expands that discourse. Indeed, in 2022, Lamar selected Accra, Ghana for the release of his album *Mr. Morale & the Big* Steppers; in hosting his release party in West Africa and collaborating on a documentary about Accra, Lamar brought visibility to that part of the world while drawing a connection between the experiences of African Americans and those of other minoritized people worldwide.

## Capitalism

McLeod's system, which dictates that the artist doesn't sellout to commercial interests, big corporations, mainstream audiences, film and television, giant labels, merchandizing, etc., seems to comport with folk authenticity discussed above. Yet, while Bob Dylan conjures images of a humble troubadour, authenticating himself through his outsider status in mainstream capitalism, hip-hop artists often position themselves in the center of consumer culture with conspicuous consumption and a celebration of material wealth. Hip-hop's relationship to capitalism must be viewed in the context of the racist history of its country of origin, extending back to the human economy of slavery, and stretching forward to the post-Civil-Rights era in places like the Bronx. In Akilah Folami's words,

> Historically, Hip-hop arose out of the ruins of a post-industrial and ravaged South Bronx, as a form of expression of urban Black and Latino youth, who politicians and the dominant public and political discourse had written off, and, for all intent and purposes, abandoned.[22]

In the South Bronx, the statistics are sobering, as predominately black and brown communities lost:

> 600,000 manufacturing jobs; 40 percent of the sector disappeared. By the mid-seventies, average per capita income dropped to $2,430, just half of the New York City average and 40 percent of the nationwide average. The official youth unemployment rate hit 60 percent. Youth advocates said that in some neighborhoods the true number was closer to 80 percent.[23]

By the mid-seventies, a third of New York's Hispanic households and a quarter of all black households were at or below the poverty line.

A rapper's material success emblematizes their transition from an object of a dysfunctional capitalist system to one of its most central subjects. Success in the rap game also exhibits an essential workaround for communities of color, who have faced racist obstacles to traditional pathways to material success in American society. Lamar's reviewers strike a delicate balance between traditional authenticating strategies, framing him as a "relic of the mid-aughts rap blog era, where bedroom WordPress pages would post zips of albums by amateurs," and an acknowledgment of Lamar's mainstream success: "By 2011, he was considering signing with Dr. Dre; by 2013, he was playing 'SNL' and touring with Kanye West."[24]

The consideration of authenticity in hip-hop leads to the last tenet of authenticity in music more generally:

**Politics may inform expressions of authenticity in music.**

Notwithstanding the political dimensions discussed above, for one *DAMN.* critic, it's Lamar's originality and sincerity that render him virtually peerless in the rap community:

> Throughout it all, he's avoided the boxed-in fates of predecessors like Nas and peers like J. Cole through an electric originality and curiosity. He mastered rap not for mastery's sake, but to use it as a form, undeterred by slow-eared fans who'll only highlight his "simplest lines."[25]

Authenticity indeed means different things in different cultural and historical contexts and therefore the authenticating strategies of an artist are aligned to genre and style period (which are themselves delineated by means of culture). Examining the cultural roots, developments within the genre, political resonances, and connections to mainstream culture provides essential insights into authenticity in the realm of popular music. Hip-hop strains traditional notions of authenticity in popular music, as many of its central tenets, storytelling, hyperreal, globalization, and conspicuous capitalism, situate it squarely within the aesthetic and philosophy of postmodernism—the subject of Chapter 3.

**Chapter Summary**

No concept is more central or contested in musical aesthetics than authenticity. Authenticity underwrites any evaluation of music, and yet its terms and conditions are multivalent. Indeed, the criteria of authenticity for a performance of a J.S. Bach sonata are entirely different from those for a Nirvana song. Moreover, a painting can be deemed nominally authentic if its origins, providence, and authorship are uncontested. A performance of a J.S. Bach sonata, however, must reckon with the meaning inscribed in the score, the presumed intentions of the composer, the technologies and cultures of the time, and the contemporary performance context. Claims of inauthenticity may refer to art that is forged, commodified, insincere, derivative, historically inaccurate, unfaithful to the score (or composer's intentions), or even simply popular. This chapter introduces the reader to central tenets of authenticity in music and invites them to grapple with the often-permeable boundary between the authentic and the inauthentic domains. The main points of the chapter are as follows:

- Authenticity is central to music criticism and aesthetics.
- Authenticity means different things in different contexts, and some of these meanings are contradictory.

- Across different contexts, five tenets of authenticity in music persist:
  - There are no attributes of musical artists or works that are universally designated authentic.
  - Authenticity is not in itself an aesthetic category, but it shapes our aesthetic responses and evaluations.
  - Mass culture, pop culture, consumer culture, and celebrity culture are almost always foils for authentic expression, which is rooted in community and/or individual experience.
  - The dictates of authenticity, even within a culture or genre, change over time.
  - Politics may inform expressions of authenticity in music.
- Authenticity can also be achieved through ironic means.
- Contemporary popular forms such as mash-ups, cover songs, and samples occupy an ambivalent space in the discourse of authenticity.
- Postmodern aesthetics, introduced in Chapter 3, challenges the tenets of authenticity.

## Guide Questions

1. Why is authenticity in music so difficult to define?
2. What artists and artistic qualities do you consider to be authentic? Inauthentic? Why?
3. In what ways does hip-hop strain traditional notions of authenticity? In what ways does the genre align with them? How can we make sense of the genre's complex relationship to discourses of authenticity?
4. Listen to Moreschi's Bach/Gounod "Ave Maria" on your preferred streaming site. What are your impressions of the piece? Do you respond similarly to the reviewers noted in the chapter? Why or why not?
5. What is the value of the hyperreal as form of artistic engagement? What are the dangers in engaging with art in this way?

## Notes

1 Casey Ellis, Amazon review of the CD release, Alessandro Moreschi, *The Last Castrato: Complete Vatican Recordings*, United States, January 27, 2002.
2 Neil G. Croll, Amazon review of the CD release, Alessandro Moreschi, *The Last Castrato: Complete Vatican Recordings*, United States, September 2, 2001.
3 Benjamin Cox, III, Amazon review of the CD release, Alessandro Moreschi, *The Last Castrato: Complete Vatican Recordings*, United States, August 19, 2004.
4 Casey Ellis, Ibid.
5 *Oxford English Dictionary*, s.v. "authenticity, n.," July 2023, https://doi.org/10.1093/OED/9125673299
6 Mering Carson, "Victorinox: Inspired by Authenticity Campaign," Summer 2022, accessed May 15, 2022, www.meringcarson.com/victorinox-swiss-army-timepieces.

## 52  Aesthetic Foundations

7. Brian Howe, "Elephant Micah: Genericana Album Review," *Pitchfork*, August 7, 2018, accessed June 1, 2024, https://pitchfork.com/reviews/albums/elephant-micah-genericana/.
8. Allan Jones, "Elephant Micah, *Genericana*," *Uncut*, August 3, 2018, accessed June 1, 2024, https://www.uncut.co.uk/reviews/elephant-micah-genericana-106716/.
9. Robin Smith, "Elephant Micah, *Genericana*," *Norman Records*, August 1, 2018, accessed June 15, 2024, https://www.normanrecords.com/records/171664-elephant-micah-genericana.
10. Sarah Lay, "Elephant Micah, *Genericana*," *Loud and Quiet*, July 31, 2018, accessed July 12, 2024, https://www.loudandquiet.com/reviews/elephantmicah-genericana/.
11. Kembrew McLeod, "Authenticity within Hip-Hop and Other Cultures Threatened with Assimilation," *Journal of Communication* 49, no. 4 (1999): 145.
12. M. Burke, "Spice 1: Evolution of a G," *The Source*, 1997, 71; quoted in McLeod, Ibid.
13. Lisa Robinson, "The Gospel According to Kendrick Lamar," *Vanity Fair*, June 28, 2018, accessed July 2, 2024, https://www.vanityfair.com/style/2018/06/kendrick-lamar-cover-story.
14. Matthew Trammell, "Kendrick Lamar: DAMN. Album Review," *Pitchfork*, April 18, 2017, accessed July 2, 2024, https://pitchfork.com/reviews/albums/23147-damn/.
15. Ibid.
16. As quoted by Alex Ross, "Here's Kendrick Lamar's *DAMN*. In Reverse Order, as Kendrick Intended It," *Vice*, August 25, 2017.
17. Mickey Hess, "Hip-Hop Realness and the White Performer," *Critical Studies in Media Communication* 22, no. 5 (2005): 372–373, 381.
18. Ibid., 381.
19. Marcus J. Moore, *The Butterfly Effect: How Kendrick Lamar Ignited the Soul of Black America* (New York: Simon and Schuster, 2021), 147.
20. Trammell, Ibid.
21. Grant Shreve, "Kendrick Lamar and Black Israelism," *JSTOR Daily*, May 7, 2018, https://daily.jstor.org/kendrick-lamar-and-black-israelism/
22. Akilah N. Folami, "From Habermas to 'Get Rich or Die Trying': Hip Hop, The Telecommunications Act of 1996, and the Black Public Sphere," *Michigan Journal of Race and Law*, Vol. 12 (Queens, NY: St. John's University School of Law, 2007), 240.
23. Jeff Chang and D.J. Kook Herc, *Can't Stop Won't Stop: A History of the Hip Hop Generation* (New York: St. Martin's Press, 2005), 13.
24. Trammell, Ibid.
25. Ibid.

# 3 Beyond Authenticity

Helene Hegemann is a contemporary German playwright and author who published her first novel, *Axolotl Roadkill* (2010), which was a critical and commercial success, at the age of sixteen. Just as the novel ascended to the top ten on a number of prominent German bestseller lists, Hegemann became mired in controversy over connections that a German blogger identified between her novel and a lesser-known German work called *Strobo*—connections that mounted concerns about plagiarism.

It thus came to light that Hegemann used an entire page of text from *Strobo*, changing only a few incidental words, as well as drawing from other unattributed sources. Confronted with charges of plagiarism, Hegemann responded by claiming that she is the voice of a new generation, one that mixes and matches content freely across media, genre, and time-period. What, in another age, might have been condemned as a bald example of plagiarism was in this case met with confusion and even some support. The book was among the top ten novels to sell on the German Amazon site in the year following the controversy.

Why is Hegemann's plagiarism not cut and dry? In large part, this is because Hegemann lives in a time of broad skepticism about easy binaries between truth and falsehood, right and wrong, author and audience; skepticism that is characteristic of postmodernism.

## Postmodernism

Beginning in the later twentieth century, critics, philosophers, and cultural theorists observed a shift in the style and concepts that governed the arts and their criticism, which was marked by a broad skepticism of truth and other grand narratives. Truth and falsehood comprise one of a number of conceptual binaries that framed intellectual thought from the Age of Enlightenment, all the way into the twentieth century. True and false; right and wrong; beautiful and ugly; real and imaginary. These naturalized oppositions began to come under scrutiny throughout the US and Europe,

DOI: 10.4324/9780429505171-5

beginning in the postwar era. The scrutiny gradually developed its own doctrine, which coalesced into the era of postmodernism. The term "postmodernism" first entered the philosophical discourse in 1979, with the publication of *The Postmodern Condition* by Jean-François Lyotard (*La Condition Postmoderne: Rapport sur le Savoir*). Although postmodernism is inherently slippery and confounds simple definitions, scholars such as Susan Sontag and Ihab Hassan extend some parameters for engaging with postmodernism and postmodern art.

Postmodernism, as a cultural, political, and artistic movement, is characterized by skepticism and relativism; "a general suspicion of reason; and an acute sensitivity to the role of ideology in asserting and maintaining political and economic power."[1] If postmodernism sounds like a rather straightforward denial of the modernist framework described above, that's because, in some sense, it is. Postmodernism is both an outgrowth of and reaction against modernism, with its tenets of authenticity and truth. Woven through the central characteristics of postmodernism are shadow concepts of modernism, now cast as naïve and simplistic. In fact,

> **Postmodernism is frequently defined in opposition to central tenets of Modernism. These include realism, truth, progress, logic, nature and learning, language, knowledge, and grand narratives.**

### *Realism*

Whereas modernists believe in an objective reality that is both outside of and observable by the human mind and its empirical techniques, postmodernists see the notion of external reality as an artificial construct, a product of language and scientific methods.

### *Truth*

Modernists believe that truth and falsehood can be objectively and scientifically ascertained. Postmodernists, by contrast, view truth as fundamentally subjective and constructed.

### *Progress*

Modernists hold that advances in science and technology will yield a more humane and prosperous society. Postmodernists may perceive such faith in science and technology as naïve and misguided, pointing to the myriad ways that they have been used (particularly instruments of war) to oppress, harm, and destroy humans and human societies.

## Logic

Whereas modernists view logic as objective and external, postmodernists see logic and other forms of reasoning as mental constructs, embedded within intellectual and cultural traditions.

## Nature versus Nurture

Consistent with the tenets above, postmodernists reject the notion that certain faculties, dispositions, and tendencies inhere in humans from birth; rather, for the postmodernist, all aspects of human psychology are learned.

## Language

Language marks one of the most decisive fault lines between modernism and postmodernism. Whereas for the modernist words accurately represent and, in this sense, mirror objects and events in the external world (e.g., table refers unproblematically to a specific piece of furniture that exists in the external world), postmodernists, influenced in particular by the work of Ferdinand de Saussure, view language as a network of meanings that are always understood in relation to other meanings and words. In this sense, language is always contingent and relative, rather than discrete and fixed. Moreover, these networks of relational words and meanings are rooted in specific linguistic, geographical, historical, and ethnic communities. Consider Michele Basquiat's postmodern painting *Cabeza* (1985), in which the word, "Aopkhes," is prominently inscribed on the figure's chest. "Aopkhes" has no known meaning, thus undermining the direct unquestioned relationship between words and their signifiers.

## Knowledge

In the seventeenth century, the father of modern philosophy, Rene Descartes, famously sloganized *cogito, ergo sum*: I think, therefore I am. For Descartes and for centuries of thinkers after him, knowledge was acquired by the intellect through reason and logic. Not surprisingly, postmodernists reject the notion that the intellect can know anything with certainty, that there is, in fact, any truth to be known.

## Grand Narratives

Finally, postmodernists are suspicious of grand narratives and sweeping theories that explain how the world works. Not only are metanarratives—whether religious, historical, or scientific—naïve; they are in fact

56  Aesthetic Foundations

pernicious because of the ways that they may be used to oppress and marginalize people and groups.

Notwithstanding their differences, these eight tenets all relativize our world and our relationship to it. Relativism is a fundamental feature of postmodernism and one that provides a starting point for any postmodern inquiry.

## Postmodern Music and Its Criticism

Many of the features of postmodernism described above translate to postmodern music and its criticism. Nevertheless, operating in the domains of sound and time, music has a unique relationship to the relativism described above that warrants elucidation. Jonathan D. Kramer is one of a number of scholars to articulate key features of postmodernism in music.[2] Drawing from Kramer's system,

> **Postmodern music is not simply a repudiation of the past but has aspects of both a break and an extension.**

This is indeed the first observation that an astute listener of postmodern music will make. The towering masterpieces of the modernist era are not, as one may assume, rejected or forgotten. They are, however, engaged with in new ways. For example, Judith Weir's opera, *Armida* (2005), updates the 1581 epic poem, *La Gerusalemme liberate*, by Torquato Tasso. The revised story is set amidst the modern Middle East conflict and features contemporary technologies such as the helicopter. Not only does the opera incorporate modern technologies, it is set for one—rather than created for a traditional opera house, *Armida* was designed for television, where it premiered in 2005.

Sometimes postmodern music borrows from its own past, as in Berio's 1968 *Sinfonia*. The third movement of Berio's *Sinfonia* is comprised entirely of excerpts of music by Ravel, Stravinsky, Brahms, Mahler, Debussy, Webern, Schoenberg, Berg, Beethoven, Hindemith, Boulez, Stockhausen, and other masters. The piece stands almost as a mockery of the Romantic cult of originality and the anxiety of influence that permeates much of Western music history. The authenticity of this movement is ironical, distanced, and critical. In this sense, it is iconically postmodern. Consider this review by Zachary Woolfe of *The New York Times*, which celebrates, rather than condemns, the work's "trippy kaleidoscope" of the musical past:[3]

> "Yes," someone says near the middle of Luciano Berio's teeming "Sinfonia," "I feel the moment has come for me to look back."

And look back Berio did. "Sinfonia," written for the New York Philharmonic at the fiery end of the 1960s, has at its center an explosive collage of past music: Mahler (a lot), Ravel, Debussy, Stravinsky, Beethoven, Strauss. Woven in with texts academic, poetic and everyday, the sounds rush together in an exuberant bouquet of fragments. The feeling is of dancing atop, and within, a trippy kaleidoscope pointed at the past.

"Sinfonia"—dedicated to Leonard Bernstein, the Philharmonic's music director at the time of its 125th anniversary, the occasion for Berio's commission—is written for eight voices and a grand orchestra. It's an early icon of affectionate postmodernism: a vision of history as bulwark, not just burden, and an attempt to render the unrest of its times explicitly as the outgrowth of what came before.

Chaotically elegant and joyfully bubbly, but unwieldy, the work doesn't get uncorked all that often. So there's ample reason to get to David Geffen Hall this weekend for a set of performances by the orchestra that played it first. (Through Saturday evening only: Get on it!)

Led here by Semyon Bychkov—a longtime friend of Berio, who died in 2003 — "Sinfonia" isn't all whimsy. Apart from that riotous patchwork third of its five movements, it's often more soberly unsettled in feel. Within its erratic textures, the vocal octet (here the flexible Roomful of Teeth, in its Philharmonic debut) makes chattering, drooping, bending sounds, and speaks texts by Samuel Beckett and the anthropologist Claude Lévi-Strauss.

In the second section, "O King," a slightly earlier work repurposed by Berio, the singers softly, unintelligibly enunciate the phonemes of the Rev. Dr. Martin Luther King Jr.'s name, punctuated by instrumental stabs. Written as a tribute, it became, after King's assassination, an elegy.

"But now it's done, it's over, we've had our chance," one of the vocalists says in the third section. "There was even, for a second, hope of resurrection." That captures both the witty and wistful sides of the work: It's simultaneously a wink at Mahler's "Resurrection" Symphony, which "Sinfonia" quotes extensively, and, perhaps, a poignant admission of the darkness into the which the '60s had by then fallen.

The Philharmonic gave a tight performance of the sprawling piece, set—in an inspired pairing—alongside Strauss's similarly larger-yet-more-compressed-than-life tone poem "An Alpine Symphony," an evocation of a mountain hike that moves with dizzying facility from boisterous energy to autumnal glow to pummeling darkness. Mr. Bychkov led an easygoing, unpressured—indeed, often delicate and poised—voluptuous performance, though the Philharmonic's most distinctive sound remains a hotly screaming super-loudness.

During the performance, the orchestra honored four members who have now served for 25 years, and four retirees: Mark Schmoockler, Vladimir Tsypin and Daniel Reed, all violinists, and Barbara Haws, the longtime archivist.

"This is the night where the present honors the past," Ms. Haws said from the stage. Berio concurred.

Rather than seeking to present the work as a coherent and sensical whole, this reviewer celebrates moments of unintelligibility, including its erratic textures and the sometimes-unsettling feeling of experiencing this "explosive" and "trippy" collage of the past.

Sampling in hip-hop may also be called upon to exhibit this aspect of postmodern music. Not only are style periods freely mixed in hip-hop songs; genres and even intended meanings may be juxtaposed, irreverently and sometimes ironically. For example, a rap song might mix the *Sesame Street* theme melody with a song about the perils of inner city gang culture or Billie Holiday's harrowing "Strange Fruit" with lyrics about a cheating spouse.

**Postmodern music is, on some level and in some way, ironic.**

One of the most iconic artifacts of postmodern popular music, The Beatles' *Sgt. Pepper's Lonely Hearts Club Band* album, exhibits the centrality of irony to this era's music. A prominent example concerns the band's engagement with live versus studio music. The album was cut in a studio and features many elements that would not be reproducible in a live context, such as double tracking and tape effects. And yet, the album presents itself as the live album of a fictional band, *The Lonely Hearts Club Band* (replete with clap tracks and recorded laughter). The ironic "liveness" of The Beatles' most processed and technologically oriented album to date, layered on top of the ironic performativity of the fictional band, paved the way for the "album era" of rock n roll, in which releases became increasingly cerebral, self-important, and aesthetically challenging.

**Postmodern music questions the mutual exclusivity of elitist and populist values and avoids totalizing forms.**

Contemporary music provides no shortage of examples of this blurring or blending of high and low, art and popular, Western and non-Western. So prominent is this tendency in music that one postmodern composer refers to postmodernism as "the age of convergence." Consider, for example, the music of Osvaldo Golijov, whose work combines elements of Western

*Figure 3.1* Beatles, *Sergeant Pepper's Lonely Hearts Club Band* Album Cover, 1967

classical traditions (from various time periods) with Argentinian tango and other popular styles. In his 2023 review of Golijov's "Falling Out of Time," *Boston Classical Review* critic, Jonathan Blumhofer, emphasizes the stylistic and generic plurality of the work and the "mystery and wonder" of its coherence:[4]

> Scored for three singers and an amplified ensemble, the piece is based on David Grossman's novel about a father coming to terms with the death of his son. Premiered by Silk Road Ensemble in 2019, *Falling Out of Time* is often predictably dark, intense and searing. Yet the score also features—despite its heavy subject matter—music of enchanting beauty and constant invention.

Much of this unfolds in the writing for the instrumental group. Here, across nearly 90 minutes, Golijov weaves his way through a bewildering variety of musical reference points and genres: drifting vocalizations; cool jazz riffs; echoes of funk, blues, rock, EDM, near-Eastern music, and more. Through all of it—the stylistic alleyways and switchbacks that are fascinating to hear as one follows Golijov's line of thought—the composer also doesn't hesitate to push instruments to their limits or present them in fresh contexts.

Though billed as multicultural, the song cycle's orchestration is largely traditional, with the only non-Western scoring involving a kamancheh (a bowed traditional Persian instrument). Golijov uses the last sparingly but memorably: its most noteworthy appearance comes in "Go Now," where kamancheh and violin engage in a lengthy, impassioned, quasi-improvisatory duet.

Also fresh and wildly unpredictable is Golijov's writing for percussion, especially the drum kit, which lets loose at a couple of points with some extended, John Bonham-worthy explosions. In one of them, the instrument even engages in a duet with an amplified violin.

How all of this holds together and coheres is the mystery and wonder of Golijov's craft. And yet, the composer's handling of his musical materials is deeply intentional: the score culminates in a movement called "Ayeka (Where Are You?)," in which instruments and voices let loose in a swooning, darkly jazzy moment of cathartic release.

**Postmodern music shows disdain for the often-unquestioned value of structural unity.**

A Mozart sonata presents itself to the ear as a model of unity and ordered perfection. One hears the eight-bar phrases floating by, and transitions are seamless. Unity was indeed a fundamental principle of the neoclassicism that Mozart and his eighteenth-century colleagues observed. A postmodern composer, on the other hand, might regard such unity as trite, naïve, or even dishonest. In postmodern music, one comes to expect the unexpected, as in Stephen Reich's *WTC 9/11*, which articulates the complicated and sometimes contradictory emotional tenor of the 9/11 terrorist attacks on the World Trade Center with a live string quartet, accompanied (and sometimes intruded) by taped sounds. The unfolding music, at once continuous and fragmented, captures the traumatic aftermath of the attacks, which continues to haunt an entire generation.

In the visual arts, similarly, unity is forfeited in the postmodern era for a constructive, aesthetic discontinuity. James Gill's 1999 *Marilyn in the*

## Beyond Authenticity

*Sky* provides an instructive example of fragmentation in postmodern studio art. Two distinct and unified sets of images are superimposed here to undermine the cohesiveness of each.

> Postmodern music considers music not as autonomous but as relevant to cultural, social, and political contexts; and, as such, includes quotations of or references to music of many traditions and cultures.

Beyond the many examples of musical quotation and allusion already mentioned, the Canadian composer, John Oswald, has coined the term "plunderphonics" to describe his process of creating musical works by sampling other recognizable songs. This style and genre is also sometimes referred as "Audio Piracy as a Compositional Prerogative" in which sound collage, drawn from music, news, educational films, and other diverse sources of audio, provides a critique of both autonomous music and music as commodity. In 1985, Oswald presented his ideas about copyright and piracy—ideas that remain relevant today—in a poetic statement to the Wired Society at the Electroacoustic Conference in Toronto:[5]

> Some of you, current and potential samplerists, are perhaps curious about the extent to which you can legally borrow from the ingredients

*Figure 3.2* James Francis Gill, *Marilyn in the Sky*, 1999
Source: Photo Credit NORPpA (Talk I Contribs)

of other people's sonic manifestations. Is a musical property properly private, and if so, when and how does one trespass upon it? Like myself, you may covet something similar to a particular chord played and recorded singularly well by the strings of the estimable Eastman Rochester Orchestra on a long-deleted Mercury Living Presence LP of Charles Ives' Symphony #3, itself rampant in unauthorized procurements. Or imagine how invigorating a few retrograde Pygmy (no slur on primitivism intended) chants would sound in the quasi-funk section of your emulator concerto. Or perhaps you would simply like to transfer an octave of hiccups from the stock sound library disk of a Mirage to the spring-loaded tape catapults of your Melotron.

Can the sounding materials that inspire composition be sometimes considered compositions themselves? Is the piano the musical creation of Bartolommeo Cristofori (1655–1731) or merely the vehicle engineered by him for Ludwig Van and others to manoeuver through their musical territory? Some memorable compositions were created specifically for the digital recorder of that era, the music box. Are the preset sounds in today's sequencers and synthesizers free samples, or the musical property of the manufacturer? Is a timbre any less definably possessable than a melody? A composer who claims divine inspiration is perhaps exempt from responsibility to this inventory of the layers of authorship. But what about the unblessed rest of us?

Let's see what the powers that be have to say. 'Author' is copyrightspeak for any creative progenitor, no matter if they program software or compose hardcore. To wit: "An author is entitled to claim authorship and to preserve the integrity of the work by restraining any distortion, mutilation or other modification that is prejudicial to the author's honor or reputation." That's called the 'right of integrity' and it's from the Canada Copyright Act. A recently published report on the proposed revision of the Act uses the metaphor of land owners' rights, where unauthorized use is synonymous with trespassing. The territory is limited. Only recently have sound recordings been considered a part of this real estate.

**Postmodern music considers technology not only as a way to preserve and transmit music but also as deeply implicated in the production and essence of music.**

As discussed above, Plunderphonics (like sampling in hip-hop) uses technology—beyond its traditional application in musical recording and transmission—as a creative tool. In this review of Carl Stone's recent releases, *Baroo* and *Himalaya*, the author refers to him as a "musical excavator" rather than composer. The result, however, is far from derivative, as Stone is seen to bring new meaning to existing musical works:[6]

American composer Carl Stone has been making sample-based music for decades, but his recent albums *Baroo* and *Himalaya* (his first solo releases in 12 years) show that he's still refining his craft. These days he primarily deals with what composer John Oswald christened "plunderphonics"—meticulously cutting up samples of music from around the world and transforming them into evocative new pieces. Stone has experimented with this technique in the past, such as on his 1990 composition "Mom's," but his latest results are far more emotive and technically impressive. Part of what makes Stone's music so fascinating is that his songs extract and magnify the specific rhythms, timbres, and moods of his source material. On "Panchita," he takes Ayumi Hamasaki's "Moments" and turns her vocals into a series of glitches, highlighting the gradual swells in her melodies through rigorous fragmentation. On "Han Yan," Stone shreds joyful Congolese guitar melodies into a million bits, but thanks to his ingenious edits, their ebullient charm still comes through. On the final two songs of *Himalaya*, he sets aside this method of precise deconstruction in favor of long-form drones: on its title track, one of the most mesmerizing pieces in Stone's oeuvre, vocalist Akaihirume patiently recites lyrics in a clear, resounding operatic timbre that foregrounds the simple power of the human voice. No matter what his methodology, Stone is an excellent musical excavator, unearthing new beauty from whatever work he touches.

**Postmodern music locates meaning and even structure in listeners, more than in scores, performances, or composers.**

Aleatoric music provides among the most overt examples of this relinquishing of authorial control. Aleatoric music refers to music that leaves some element of the unfolding soundscape unspecified or up to chance. In 1951, John Cage, for example, adapted the ancient Chinese *I-Ching* method of tossing coins to determine outcomes as a compositional tool in his *Music of Changes;* in the forward to the score, Cage notes that in places "the notation is irrational; in such instances, the performer is to employ [their] discretion." Aleatoric elements such as these result in a unique, indeterminate musical composition each time the piece is played, thus forfeiting the sanctity of the work, the autonomy of the author, and (sometimes) the authority of the score.

### Postmodernism in a Post-Truth Era

The aesthetics of postmodernism, which have proliferated since the 1950s, take on new meanings in the contemporary era of post-truth. Post-truth is a term used since the twenty-first century to refer to the diminishing of shared,

64  *Aesthetic Foundations*

objective standards of truth and the concomitant breakdown of the distinction between facts, opinions, and beliefs. According to scholars of politics and media, post-truth rhetoric tends to feature "truthiness," a term that denotes assertions that one feels to be true and responds to emotionally rather than rationally; post-truth rhetoric obscures facts and blurs the boundaries between facts and opinions; it appeals to personal beliefs and experiences; and it capitalizes on strong negative emotions such as anger, resentment, and outrage.

Post-truth controversies most often revolve around competing versions of politicized events in the news, and some post-truth art uses postmodern aesthetics to engage with it. For example, Jeff Bartels' *Alternative Artifacts: Strange Antiques from the Post Truth World*, offers a series of post-truth realism paintings that feature hyperreal images of artifacts that never existed. The series is seen to manipulate the truth of our past in order to raise awareness of deceptions in the political sphere. The artist statement explicitly connects the aesthetic and political realms:[7]

> Each antique is surrounded by a simple background which removes any point of reference for the viewer to hold on to. This singular focus on the object and nothing else mirrors the practice of cherry-picking facts in order to push a falsehood. The meaning behind the series is purposefully opaque when initially viewing the paintings. The viewer isn't aware that the whole point of the collection is to mislead them. The objects vary from silly and nonsensical like a diving helmet wearing headphones or a motorcycle powered by a French horn to darker and more disturbing like a corkscrew syringe or tattoo drill. The one thing they all have in common is that none of them are real, they are all fake.

*Figure 3.3* Jeff Bartels, *Alternative Artifacts: Strange Antiques from the Post Truth World*, 2021

In other cases, however, pernicious truthiness in the political sphere has given rise to a return among cultural producers to themes of sincerity, hope, and honesty. This post-postmodernist turn, which can be seen in literature, film, music, and art, has roots in (among other places) the so-called new sincerity of a group of Austin-based musicians in the 1980s, who turned away from the irony and cynicism that dominated the mainstream music world of that time. Today, one can find elements of diversity and relativism associated with postmodernism alongside appeals to honesty and authenticity that reflect a new era. Like all new eras, however, post-postmodernism will reveal itself most clearly in retrospect; by that time, perhaps we will be living in a post-post-postmodern world.

## Chapter Summary

The third movement of Berio's *Sinfonia* is comprised entirely of excerpts of music by Ravel, Stravinsky, Brahms, Mahler, Debussy, Webern, Schoenberg, Berg, Beethoven, Hindemith, Boulez, Stockhausen, and other masters. The piece stands almost as a mockery of the Romantic cult of originality and the anxiety of influence that permeates much of Western music history. The authenticity of this movement is ironical, distanced, and critical. In this sense, it is iconically postmodern. The term "postmodernism" first entered the philosophical discourse in 1979, with the publication of *The Postmodern Condition* by Jean-François Lyotard. Although postmodernism is inherently slippery and confounds simple definitions, scholars extend some parameters for engaging with postmodernism and postmodern music. The main points of the chapter are as follows:

- Postmodernism was coined by Jean-François Lyotard in 1979.
- Postmodern aesthetics undermines some of the traditional tenets of authenticity.
- Postmodernism defies definition; however, cultural theorists and philosophers have outlined some of its pervasive features. In music, these include
  - A concern with popular and non-Western forms of expression
  - A breakdown of rigid distinctions between art and entertainment, composer and performer (and listener), score and sound, art and commodity
  - An embrace of active, ritual, practical, and embodied musical expressions and experiences
  - An acknowledgment of the social, economic, and political meanings and functions of music
  - A rejection of unitary meanings and definitions
  - An embrace of surface and simulacrum
- Postmodern music criticism reflects these values and embraces these features in musical works.

- Relativizing truth can have negative consequences, and post-postmodernism features a backlash against the irony and cynicism that pervaded postmodern art (including music) and literature.

## Guide Questions

1. Why do you think postmodernism (like post-postmodernism) carries forth the term modernism in its name?
2. Why is irony an important feature of postmodern art? What is changed in communicated something ironically (as opposed to directly)?
3. What is the relationship between postmodernism and post-truth? Should artists be operating on the fault line between truth and falsehood at a time of broad culture skepticism?
4. Is plunderphonics art? Is it original? Why or why not?
5. What is the aesthetic value of musical borrowing; are there similarities between the borrowings of Berio on the one hand and hip-hop samples on the other?

## Notes

1 B. Duignan, "Postmodernism," *Encyclopedia Britannica*, accessed July 29, 2023, www.britannica.com/topic/postmodernism-philosophy.
2 Jonathan D. Kramer, *Postmodern Music, Postmodern Listening*, edited by Robert Carl (New York: Bloomsbury Publishing, 2016).
3 Zachary Woolfe, "Review: The Philharmonic Points a Trippy Kaleidoscope at the Past," *New York Times*, May 25, 2018, accessed June 24, 2022, https://www.nytimes.com/2018/05/25/arts/music/review-new-york-philharmonic-berio-sinfonia.html.
4 Jonathan Blumhofer, "Osvaldo Golijov's Masterful 'Falling Out of Time' Lights a Path Through Grief," *Boston Classical Review*, May 1, 2023, accessed February 4, 2024, https://bostonclassicalreview.com/2023/05/osvaldo-golijovs-masterful-falling-out-of-time-illuminates-a-path-through-grief/.
5 John Oswald, "Plunderphonics, or Audio Piracy as a Compositional Prerogative," *Musicworks* 34 (1985).
6 Joshua Minsoo Kim, "Carl Stone's Sample-Based Compositions Unearth New Beauty Hidden in Other People's Music," *Chicago Reader*, September 5, 2019, accessed April 2, 2022, https://chicagoreader.com/music/carl-stones-sample-based-compositions-unearth-new-beauty-hidden-in-other-peoples-music/.
7 Jeff Bartels, Artist Statement for "Alternative Artifacts: Strange Antiques from the Post Truth World," *Jeff Bartels: Post Truth Realism*, 2021, accessed June 4, 2022, https://www.jeffbartels.com/alternativeartifacts.

# Part 2
# Criticizing Music

# 4 Describing Music

> The study "Winter Trees," was created by Egon Schiele, with oil and soft pencil on canvas, in 1912. As the title suggests, the trees are bare. A stick protrudes from the ground beside each tree. On the far left side of the horizon line, the viewer will observe a blue smudge. On the other side of the image, tangled in the branches, one sees a string of barbed wire. Despite this coarse intrusion, the image is, on the whole, a pastoral one, depicting nature with cheerful specks of colorful and a big enveloping sky.

Most of us would agree that this description of Schiele's 1912 "Winter Trees" fails to orient the reader or generate a meaningful connection to the piece. But why? Where did the critic go wrong? Defined as an oral or written account of a person, object, or event, the simplest definition of *description* does little to reveal the principles that guide effective critical work. Examining the failures of this description brings to light elements and characteristics of description that can be applied to music criticism.

**Descriptions direct us to relevant matter and away from irrelevant matter.**

Perhaps most glaringly in the description above, poor descriptions include obvious and extraneous information. Any of the events contained in the description could have been developed to communicate meaning, but as it stands, they were left dangling and confused. The blue smudge, the barbed wire, the sticks protruding from the ground—none of these details supports the characterization of the study as "cheerful" or "pastoral," and as such they distract the reader from the meaning that is intended. Effective descriptions do not endeavor to include all information that is needed to "know" the object or event being described; rather, they provide curated details that support a particular experience of their own. Consider this description of "Night Visions," from Watain's *The Wild Hunt*, which operates alongside the song as a companion experience:[1]

DOI: 10.4324/9780429505171-7

*Figure 4.1* Egon Schiele, *Winterbäume* (Winter Trees), 1912

This is far from the near-instant explosion of "Death's Cold Dark" that opened the previous LP *Lawless Darkness*. "Night Visions" is a far more considered affair, more of an instrumental tone-setter that, as it unfurls, seems to suggest that what you are about to experience is more than just a mere collection of songs—it's an incantation that summons open the gateway to Watain's world and beckons you to journey inside. It's epic yet brooding, as first decidedly mournful and bleak guitar picking bursts into tidal swells of noise which sweep and pulsate, conjuring the sort of cyclonic atmosphere one presumably senses when approaching the Black Gate of Mordor.

This evocative and imagistic description uses the song as a launchpad for the construction of "Watain's world," which is rich in emotion. The entire description is founded on metaphors, which do not so much pull you into the music as alongside it. The purpose here is not to obviate a hearing of the song through the description; on the contrary, the purpose is to describe it in a way that is so rich as to compel the reader to listen to the song.

This description of DJ Kahled's "Jealous" similarly uses only the choicest and hardest working metaphors:[2]

> With trap savant Tay Keith commanding the production, the song is a vibrant earworm destined to crawl its way into the Hot 100. Aside from Brown's catchy chorus, Wayne's Auto-Tune sing-song delivery and Sean's punchy verse should help "Jealous" sprint into the playlists of lovesick fans.

Though succinct, this description offers a vivid portrayal of the song it characterizes: we know from the description that "Jealous" is a catchy, pop-oriented love song, with trap beats and processed vocals. Words like "punchy" and "vibrant" give us a clear sense of the song's affect, and although the critic offers no specifics about the sound profile of the chorus, we know that it will get stuck in our heads, which gives us any number of pop songs to compare it to. To be sure, this critic could add additional details to this description—specific lyrics, details about the tempo, length, instrumentation, etc.—but without contextualization, they would only muddle this selective and targeted account of the song.

**Descriptions invite the reader into a particular way of experiencing the object or event. They are in some sense persuasive.**

The critic tells us that the Schiele study is pastoral, cheerful even. This is in essence how they want us to interpret the image, and yet the description that precedes that determination does not compel us to experience it as such. The gray sky, barbed wire, bare trees—none of these features coalesces around the characterization "cheerful." Effective descriptions present the object or event in a way that deepens our connection to the piece. By this nature, its work is to orient the listener or reader and to give them purchase on the critic's views. Here is Anna Wood's description of "Signs of Life," from Arcade Fire's album, *Everything Now*, which invites the reader into a specific way of experiencing the piece:

> Yes always to bass and handclaps. No never to a huffy bloke who thinks he's wry and wise when he tells you about how staying out late every night is bad ("Love is hard, sex is easy," he says. You're doing it wrong, mate). This is mean-spirited conservatism that thinks it's edgy and cool,

with the added bonus of sexist undertones; you think you've got it all worked out, kids, but soon you'll realise that you should be sticking it to the man by writing anodyne pop songs, drinking kombucha and getting to bed early. To add insult to insult, they nick squelchy 70s basslines and sci-fi strings from a culture where sex and staying up late were part of the glorious orthodoxy. There is a good bit near the end though where it starts to sound a bit like "Thriller."[3]

The tension between sound and substance is established at the outset. For Wood, the seventies basslines, handclaps, and sci-fi string accompaniment are foils for the "mean-spirited" sexist conservatism projected by the lyrics. With this description, Wood invites the reader to focus on the latter and thus offers a clear—and well-defended—point of view for the reader to engage with.

**Descriptions are subjective (in that they emphasize some details and omit others); however, they are networked to observable or objective features of the object or event.**

Is that jagged line on the left side of the canvas indeed barbed wire? Most of us would agree that it is not. To be sure, a connection could be made between the rough line of the bare horizontal branch and an imposing stretch of barbed wire; but the claim that the line is intended to be perceived as barbed wire itself is not defensible. The reader loses confidence in a description that does not correspond to one's own perceptions. From this perspective, effective descriptions are authoritative. They reflect a studied, knowledgeable, and intelligent engagement with the work being described. We certainly don't care to read about every pause, drum-kick, and quarter note of a piece of music at hand. However, effective descriptions are supported by concrete, observable details. Consider, for example, this description of "How To Draw/Petrichor," by The 1975, which, though it presents a point of view, is nevertheless grounded in observable details:

> It really feels like "How To Draw/Petrichor" has a life of its own. If you listen carefully you can hear it inhaling and exhaling. Just shy of six minutes, delicate embers of sound inform the first half. It's a transcendent and ethereal mixture of noises almost reminiscent of a child's soothing nursery toy before a sonic metamorphosis exaggerates the fuzzy electronics the band have already experimented with alongside some spiky ska and garage inflects thrown in for good measure. It pushes and pulls you but ultimately immerses you into the dynamic production from Matty and George.[4]

Selective in the extreme, this description nevertheless gives the uninitiated reader a satisfying grounding in the music's sound world: its six minutes are divided more or less into two halves. The first half features "delicate embers" of "soothing," ethereal noises. In the second half, the embers become flames as the synthesized noises are "exaggerated" and combined with ska and garage inflections. Although the suggestions of children's toys and fuzzy electronics give the sense of a highly processed, artificial soundscape, the author paints a convincing portrait of organicism: the inhales and exhales; the dynamism, and the gradual metamorphoses all support the critic's observation that the song seems to have "a life of its own."

Maeve McDermott's review of Nicki Minaj's "Chun Swae" (featuring Swae Lee), from the album, *Queen*, is similarly targeted and persuasive:

> This song definitely didn't need to be six minutes long, but there's something hypnotic about producer Metro Boomin's plinking beat, sounding like a deranged music box with Swae Lee's boy-choir falsetto and Minaj's baby-voiced rapping. Just press skip before the song reaches its lengthy and unnecessary outro.[5]

The choice adjectives in this description work overtime. Plinking, for example, refers to informal target shooting that features non-traditional targets such as tin cans and soda bottles. The word, which employs onomatopoeia, points to the sharp, metallic sound that that a successful shot may produce. The image of the "deranged music box" is similarly evocative, as it provides a novel, but almost universally comprehensible way to hold the sound. Once again, though the reader is left with a clear impression of the critic's response to the song, that response is nevertheless grounded in observable features of the music.

Returning to the Schiele study at the beginning of this chapter, one can now envision a description that offers cognitive purchase on the image and generates a sense of connection with both the work and the viewpoint of the critic. An exemplary description is offered by Rudolf Leopold:

> Bare trees standing on bare ground—a subject Schiele repeatedly addressed and treated as an allegory of life. The fragile branches and slender, crooked trunks appear absolutely helpless, as if they would fall were it not for the props. The sky is gray. A few brighter lights and the two sunlike configurations that appear on the horizon—likewise gray, but somewhat lighter in tone—do not mitigate the sense of desolation but rather amplify it by the impression of unreality they convey.
>
> The character of the textures in the sky shows a certain affinity with the drawing of the branches. On the other hand, the gestural brushwork

of the blue, reddish and ocher flecks lends little vitality to the largely unarticulated ground, these color contrasts tending rather to reinforce its appearance of sterility.[6]

On the basis of these examples, description need not stand in for the work. Rather, it invites the reader into a particular way of experiencing the work and grounds the interpretation and evaluation. An effective description stands out, not for its thoroughness but rather for its insight. It is also clear from these examples that descriptions need not be technical; however, it does help to arm oneself with some musical knowledge and vocabulary, whether or not it becomes part of the final product. Following are some basic technical tools for understanding the substance and material of music:

## Elements of Music

Before defining the elements of music, one should endeavor to define music itself. Traditionally, music was defined as a pleasing succession of tones. However, the landscape of music has expanded in recent generations to include noise, silence, speaking and screaming, environmental sounds such as honking cars and flowing water, and responses to music that transcend a narrow concept of pleasure. (Some forms of music are intended to evoke fear, pain, horror, etc.) As such, definitions of music have broadened to focus on creating, disciplining, or framing sound and silence toward the creation of art.

Both traditional and contemporary ways of defining music are accommodated by music's most elemental feature, which Arnie Cox refers to as the acoustic fact.[7] The acoustic fact comprises features of the sound that define its properties and distinguish it from other sounds. The acoustic fact acknowledges that musical sounds and silences are experienced by "embodied" listeners—or listeners with intellectual, emotional, and physical responses and reactions—and contexts in which music is created and consumed (such as concert halls and clubs, etc.). Every sound has a timbre, a duration, a strength, and a location. Many musical sounds also have pitch. Though silences contain only the property of duration, they too contribute to musical events. These are the ingredients of music, and we can consider how they interact and inform music by examining a well-known song by The Beatles, "Let it Be."

### *Timbre*

Timbre is a word of French origin, meaning "tone color." It refers to the character or quality of sounds that distinguish them from one another. It defines the distinction between the sounds produced by a piano and those produced, for example, by a saxophone. Imagine if "Let it Be" were played on kazoo rather than piano. The song could have the exact same pitches and rhythms, and yet it would sound (and feel) completely different. The difference would be a matter of timbre. Even within instrument categories, differences can be heard. This is why a guitar player might play 20 different guitars before choosing one to purchase. Similarly, human speech, though universally produced with the vocal cords, is unique to the individual, based on that person's lungs, vocal folds, larynx, and the tongue, palate, cheeks, and lips. Each of us, being physiologically unique, possesses a unique vocal timbre.

Although "spectral envelope," "amplitude modulation," and "attack and decay" all influence the timbre of the sound being produced, critics are more often drawn to metaphorical language to describe subtleties of timbre—that instrument sounds warm; that one, brassy; this one, tinny; that one, bright. Some common metaphors used to describe instrument timbre are reedy, clear, focused, unfocused, breathy, dark, round, piercing, strident, harsh, warm, mellow, resonant, heavy, light, flat, nasal, pure, dull, metallic, wooden, hollow, rich, ringing, gentle, tinny, smooth, shrill, breathy, earthy, strong, natural, turgid, and tinkling.

It is common to refer to brass instruments as bright, brassy, clear, and strident and woodwind instruments as earthy, woody, round, warm, and mellow; however, these metaphors are subjective and can be applied in unique ways to bring out subtle or undetected aspects of musical sound.

## Duration

Almost all US popular music is built on the foundation of a defining pulse, and most people can locate and clap or tap the pulse intuitively. This is largely because pulses generally unfold at a consistent rate of speed or tempo and can therefore be anticipated. Nevertheless, not all pulses are the same. Listening closely, one observes that some pulses are stronger than others, in a similar way to the iambic and dactylic patterns of poems. In music, as in poetry, these patterns of strong and weak beats constitute meter.

Most US popular music falls into groupings of four beats, in which beats one and three are strong and two and four are weak. (This is called a 4/4 meter because there are four beats per measure or unit, and a quarter note gets one beat.) However, phrases do not always begin on beat one, alternating in a tidy pattern that corresponds with the text. Consider, for example, the first line of "Let it Be." In "Let it Be," the first accented word is "find," and "When I" is situated as an upbeat, anticipating the first beat of the measure, the downbeat. Continuing, we feel strong beats on the "self" of "myself," which is beat two, on "times" and on the first syllable of "trouble," which constitute beats three and four, respectively.

As suggested, in a typical 4/4 meter (in which the pulses are oriented around groups of four), the first and third syllables will naturally feel stronger than the second and fourth. However, weak beats can be given artificial accents to tremendous effect, disrupting the natural flow of strong and weak beats, and therefore creating a pleasant sense of movement in the music (and the listener). The technical term for this type of "false accent" is "syncopation," and one of the most common and standardized types of syncopation in US popular music is the backbeat. The backbeat, which features a sustained accent on beats two and four, is so common in US popular music, that we tend not to hear it as syncopation at all. Nevertheless, by disrupting the natural beat hierarchy of the meter, the backbeat creates movement in the music, which propels the listener to an embodied experience that might be felt as a desire to dance. Although the first verse of "Let it Be" features an even pulse on the piano and only a subtle beat hierarchy supplied by the vocals, the second verse features a high-hat backbeat accent on beats two and four.

While some instruments (like drums and bass) tend to focus on producing and sustaining meter, others create more varied durations that comprise rhythm. If the song unfolded in complete agreement with the pulse, it would be monotonous to listen to. Therefore, the pulse lies underneath the flow of the tune, which unfolds over it. In "Let it Be," the tune, or melody of the song features subtle variations in durations as the words unfold. These variations constitute the rhythm and are generally not patterned.

### Strength

Just as every sound has a duration, it also has a strength, or loudness. Patterns and changes in loudness among instruments and groups of instruments constitute dynamics. Those who have had some exposure to music's technical language will be familiar with the terms *forte* and *piano*. (The terms *forte* and *piano* derive from an instrument called just that, fortepiano. It was developed in the eighteenth century and was noteworthy for its ability to project dynamics, which the harpsichord, its predecessor, could not.) These are terms used to instruct performers about how much strength to give to a specific note or note grouping. At the beginning of "Let it Be," not only is the piano playing alone, without other instruments, thus lending a quiet, sparse sound profile to the song; beyond that, the player is playing softly, or *piano*. Over the course of the unfolding song, other instruments layer over the piano, and the piano is played with increasing strength, thus creating a louder sound profile. The increasing volume of the sound impacts the affect or mood that the song projects.

## Location

As the term suggests, location denotes the sound source. Location concerns whether the sounds seem to be coming from close by or far away; left or right; above or straight ahead. Locational aspects of sound, though seemingly tangential to the music, can influence our experience of a song and the affect that it projects. Church organ pipes, from which the sound emanates, are located above and often behind the congregation, giving the effect of music emitting from the heavens. Some church choirs, similarly, are situated on balconies above the congregation so that the music seems to rain down on the congregants. In this case, the location is used to create audible metaphors that shape our responses to and experiences of the music.

One of the most famous examples of sound source manipulations is Edgard Varese's *Poeme Electronique*, which was composed for the World Fair in Brussels in 1958. The eight-minute piece was written for performance in the newly constructed Phillips Pavilion. In the pyramid shaped pavilion, upwards of 350 speakers were situated across the walls from the bottom to the top, and they were manipulated with dials, each of which controlled five speakers. The sound was thus experienced as traveling up and down the walls of the pavilion. In this case, location became an aesthetic property of the music, rather than merely a byproduct.

*Figure 4.2* Phillips Pavilion, 1958

Location is not just a feature of live music. Although the vast majority of music consumed today is mediated by technology, locational effects can be manipulated by, for example, putting some sounds in one speaker and other sounds in the other, by using effects to create an echo or sense of distance, or by adjusting dynamics to give the effect of a close or distant location.

## Pitch

When we talk about singing high notes or a person with an uncommonly deep, low voice, we are using metaphors of height to describe the differences produced by different wave frequencies of sound. Pitches constitute what we hear as "notes" in music, and when strung together with rhythm, they produce "melodies" or "tunes." Not all musical sounds are definitively pitched; for example, some percussion instruments don't seem to project notes or tunes. When we clap along to music, we don't ascribe pitch to those claps. And some forms of singing, such as rapping, seems to move along the continuum between speech and song. In "Let it Be," words being sung by John constitute the melody, which unfolds as a sequence of pitches, each with a rhythmic value. Both successions and combinations of pitches can create stability or instability; stability gives a sense of home, arrival, calmness; instability demands movement and creates an urge toward resolution. Most music needs both stability and instability, consonance and dissonance, in order to create a satisfying experience. In fact, dissonance is sometimes understood as the primary generator of musical meaning. *The Wall Street Journal* published an essay in 2012 that explained the popularity of Adele's music through the presence of a particular type of dissonance, called an appoggiatura:

> Twenty years ago, the British psychologist John Sloboda conducted a simple experiment. He asked music lovers to identify passages of songs that reliably set off a physical reaction, such as tears or goose bumps. Participants identified 20 tear-triggering passages, and when Dr. Sloboda analyzed their properties, a trend emerged: 18 contained a musical device called an "appoggiatura."[8]

The Italian word, appoggiatura, means literally, to lean upon or rest; in music, it refers to a specific type of ornament in which the melody note is displaced by a neighboring dissonance. The satisfying arrival of the melody note is delayed, which creates a pleasing sense of anticipation and (ultimately) satisfaction. As researchers noted,

> Chills often descend on listeners at these moments of resolution. When several appoggiaturas occur next to each other in a melody, it generates a cycle of tension and release. This provokes an even stronger reaction, and that is when the tears start to flow.

"Someone Like You" . . . is sprinkled with ornamental notes similar to appoggiaturas. In addition, during the chorus, Adele slightly modulates her pitch at the end of long notes right before the accompaniment goes to a new harmony, creating mini-roller coasters of tension and resolution.[9]

As this essay suggests, pitches are sequenced and combined to support the effects of tension and release. In "Let it Be," even if you don't study music theory, you can hear that the first phrase could not end on "speaking words of wisdom." Although the text phrase could satisfactorily end there, the music is left dangling and unresolved in a moment of tension and anticipation. Only when the melody descends to "Let it be" does the phrase feel musically complete.

As discussed in this section, the acoustic fact comprises timbre, location, strength, duration, and pitch. Critical descriptions do not catalog these features of music for their own sake; rather, they use a knowledge of these technical aspects of music to inform their often-metaphorical, creative, and targeted descriptions. Consider some descriptions of Billie Holiday's unique vocal quality and singing style. This one begins with considerations of Holiday's manipulation of pitch.

> One of the most distinctive features of her style was the fluctuations of pitch she used to create contrast elements in her phrasing . . . . These inflections interrupted the melody flow in such a way as to create small bursts of emotion, which served to keep the audience hanging on to each word she sang.[10]

Continuing, the critic next introduces vocal timbre and rhythm:

> Her articulation relied heavily on open ended vowel sounds, which allowed for more softened and elongated phrasing. She also took great care in the syllable-by-syllable pronunciation of the lyrics . . . . She had a unique style in the stretching of words and phrases to create swing combined with off-beat timing.[11]

Another critic acknowledges her limited pitch range and weak projection (or strength), all the while pointing to her inimitable "instrumental" musicality:[12]

> With a narrow range and weak projection, her delivery wasn't to everyone's taste; but her revolutionary approach had an insidious charm that began to win her a devoted following, not least amongst musicians, who loved her, partly because, although she could be demanding, she was one of them: she used her voice as an instrument.

Some critics, such as this one, emphasized the affect of her unique voice and delivery. Nevertheless, this critic uses a knowledge of timbre, pitch, rhythm, and meter to inform their discussion of less concrete, though deeply felt, aspects of Holiday's sound:

> Unlike, say, Bessie Smith or Ella Fitzgerald, Holiday did not have an overpowering vocal instrument. What she did have was an irresistible concept: she would command attention not with forcefulness but with reluctance. She would sing in a low-key hush, landing on the tail end of the beat, as if hesitant to reveal too much. Even when she sang a happy song, she seemed half in a dream world she wasn't sure she should share. This led her audiences to wonder: What is she hiding? Will she lose contact with the rhythm altogether? She never did, but the suspense never let up. She would allow vowels to swell with purring suggestion till the audience might wonder if her words might pop like balloons. Within that bruised purr were hints of pain, giddiness, anger, infatuation, stoicism and defiance, enticing enough to invite speculation but mysterious enough to keep the listener guessing.[13]

Here again, the discussion of meaning, feeling, and mood is grounded in the recognition of Holiday's manipulation of musical materials:

> What Holiday could do in a manner far beyond any other performer was to communicate feelings, and not just single moods, but complex emotional clusters. She could drag a few words across the beat—possibly lyrics banal in themselves—in such a manner as to convey ruefulness, irony, tenderness, love, joy, resignation, salty delight, one after another, or several all together. But to do this, you had to be Holiday. More than that, by her own account you had to be Holiday on a certain day.[14]

Despite acknowledging Holiday's physical limitations, all of these critics present commendatory descriptions of Holiday's voice and delivery. They use features of the acoustic fact to justify and deepen their explanations of her unique musical style. Through these compelling descriptions, Holiday emerges as an icon of music history.

And yet, neither Wagner, nor Verdi, nor Mozart—three of history's greatest opera composers—would have likely appreciated Holiday's voice. I know of no recordings of Schubert Lieder by Holiday; and it would be ludicrous to compare her to Ariana Grande. When these critics commend Holiday's unique vocal delivery, they do so in the context of genre.

## Genre

Do you like horror movies? Are you a sucker for romance novels? Do you know how to swing dance? Horror, romance, swing; these broad ways that we organize our tastes and preferences comprise the domain of genre, which may be defined as a system of categorizing works of art and other cultural artifacts according to similarities in form, style, and/or subject matter. The classification of art has been a central project of history and criticism since antiquity. Genre provides a meaningful organizing system for our engagement with art. In technical terms, genre distinctions are those of "class, type, or category, as sanctioned by convention."[15] As such, genres are defined and delimited through the process of repetition. That which is carried forth in a class or type (or, in other words, repeated) thus defines the generic conventions of that class or type. In this sense, genre categorizations are descriptive; however, there is no question that they are also prescriptive. That which is "sanctioned by convention" is thus carried forth by it, marking the principles and guidelines for future artistic creation. To be sure, these principles and guidelines are not rules but rather expectations, and the effective work of art possesses a just balance of expectations met and denied. Expectations denied often give rise to new subgenres, which distinguish indie rock artist, Jack White, from Mick Jagger and The Rolling Stones, and, similarly, Ornette Coleman's free jazz from the big band music of Duke Ellington.

Nevertheless, repetition remains the defining and essential principle of generic categorization. So what exactly repeats? There is no question that musical materials, sound profiles, forms, and devices are carried forth in genre; beyond these, it must be acknowledged that genres repeat or sanction social, behavioral, and ideological systems and domains. We can talk about the folk music in terms of poetic lyrics, acoustic, portable instruments, untrained vocal quality, and loose, improvisatory musical structures; however, any categorization of folk music in the US is incomplete without considering the influence of the Kerouacian beat writers, leftist political activists, and the general climate of support for racial and gender equality. In this sense, the folk genre is inscribed with both musical and cultural meanings, which are maintained and/or modified over time and across geographical systems. Genre tends to delimit the instrumentation, form, topic, style features, and general sound world of a piece of music. Generic literacy concerns recognizing and articulating the central features and distinctions between genres. Although ultimately, each work of art must be taken as unique and individual, its meaning and value are also located within a cultural and historical system that genre defines. This consideration of genre helps to explain why Billie Holiday was never hired to sing in a production of Wagner's opera, *Parsifal*. Holiday was not just an excellent singer; she was, more specifically, an excellent jazz singer.

This is not to say that jazz and opera can't mix. Sometimes discussions of genre are used to push the boundaries of our expectations and assumptions. Consider this review of Hakon Kornstad's album by Paul Bowers:

> No one ever accused Håkon Kornstad of playing it safe. A conservatory-trained tenor saxophonist who first made his name in the late '90s with the Norwegian electronic jazz band Wibutee, Kornstad has since created a wholly unique solo show with tenor and bass saxophones, flute, flutonette, and an audio-looping device.
> Now he has a new weapon in his arsenal: a formidable opera tenor.
> On paper, it's an absurd and incongruous collection of talents for one man to have. But in concert—whether with his full-band show Tenor Battle or in the daring solo show he'll bring to Spoleto—the music stuns with its beauty far more often than it befuddles with its strangeness.
> On Soundcloud, where Kornstad holds a near monopoly on the hashtagged genre description #operajazz, hours of his live recordings give a taste of the treats in store. When we get to a recording of Paolo Tosti's popular opera piece "Marechiare," Kornstad sings the old tune gracefully before launching into a saxophone improvisation based loosely around the melody. On Gluck's "O del mio dolce ardor," Kornstad opens with a gently clicking, fluttering saxophone solo that loops and builds as he starts to sing, to bewitching effect.
> Even before he learned to sing opera, Kornstad could catch an audience off guard by layering breathy drones over the subtle percussion of his saxophone's keys before improvising solos on multiple instruments in sequence. A loop pedal, long a favorite toy of bedroom guitar noodlers who like to rip solos over their own rhythms, can be a cheap party trick in some settings. But a master like Kornstad can make it a formidable instrument in its own right.
> [. . .]
> Today, Kornstad stands poised to introduce jazz—and opera—to yet another generation. What his songs lack in pop sensibility they make up for in sheer genre-bending, crowd-silencing chutzpah.[16]

## Style Period

Musical genre is further conditioned by style period, which refers to an historical period that is associated with particular musical tendencies and characteristics. "Rap music" may indeed be a genre, but that broad categorization does little to discriminate between Public Enemy and Kanye West. Folk music likewise positions nineteenth-century Polish dance songs alongside Bob Dylan and Buffie Saint Marie. Articulating the style period within a genre provides essential organizing information for any categorization or art. Nevertheless, like genres, style periods are sometimes only loosely and always retrospectively defined and delimited. In the 1980s, rock 'n' roll became "classic rock," a radio format that catered to older audiences who grew up on blues-based popular music from the '60s and '70s. "Classic rock" denotes both a genre and a style period.

## Audience

Considering the audience highlights perceived distinction between popular and classical music and also, within popular music, between indie and mainstream genres. More problematic are the broader distinctions in music and culture between art and entertainment, in no small part because they often operate along socioeconomic and racial fault lines. Is there a meaningful distinction between art and entertainment? Are they produced, respectively, for different audiences and purposes? Bill Lasarow makes this argument for the dual necessity of art and entertainment, as well as clear distinctions between them:

> Simply put, when aesthetic purpose precedes exposure and sales, art plays the upper hand. When reversed, it's about entertainment . . . . For a quick jolt of adrenaline, you can't beat Six Flags or a well made action flick. By contrast, good art demands that you slow down and be patient.[17]

Whether or not you agree with Lasarow, considering the debates about art and entertainment can inform your engagement with a piece of music in meaningful ways. Chapter 10 deals with these debates in more detail.

## Chapter Summary

This chapter draws from a selection of critical writings about music to define the central principles of musical description. It introduces and distinguishes musical genres, style periods, and contexts for consumption. The main points of the chapter are as follows:

- Music is sometimes dichotomized into art and entertainment. These distinctions are entrenched but undeniably fraught.
- Within each of these categories works may be organized by genre. Genre defines the instrumentation, form, topic, style features, and general sound world of a piece of music.
- Within genres are subgenres, each with its own features and forms.
- Different style periods have different aesthetic properties and values.

84  Criticizing Music

- Contexts for consumption center on the distinction between popular and classical music but also feature distinctions, for example, between live and studio music.
- Regardless of genre, style period, and context for consumption, all music contains some combination of the following features associated with the acoustic fact: timbre, duration, strength, location, and pitch.
- Effective descriptions are selective, targeted, purposeful, and insightful.

## Guide Questions

1. Choose five musical instruments and identify descriptive words for each one's timbre.
2. Is the distinction between art and entertainment a useful one? Why or why not?
3. Choose a piece of mainstream popular music and see if you can identify (and clap along with) the backbeat.
4. Locate (in popular magazines, newspapers, and websites) a short musical description that interests you. Analyze the description, using the discussion of effective descriptions in section one of this chapter.

## Notes

1 Toby Cook, "Watain's the Wild Hunt: A Track by Track Review," *The Quietus*, August 6, 2013, accessed January 14, 2019, https://thequietus.com/quietus-reviews/track-by-track/watain-the-wild-hunt-review/.
2 Carl Lammare, "DJ Khaled's 'Father of Asahd' Track-by-Track Review," *Billboard*, May 17, 2019, accessed February 2, 2020, https://www.billboard.com/music/rb-hip-hop/dj-khaled-father-of-asahd-track-by-track-review-8511993/.
3 Anna Wood, "Arcade Fire's Everything Now Reviewed Track by Track," *The Quietus*, July 31, 2017, accessed November 16, 2021, https://thequietus.com/quietus-reviews/track-by-track/arcade-fire-s-everything-now-reviewed-track-by-track/.
4 Shannon Cotton, "Track by Track Review: The 1975—A Brief Inquiry into Online Relationships," *Gigwise*, November 25, 2018, September 20, 2021, https://www.gigwise.com/reviews/3301770/track-by-track-review--the-1975-a-brief-inquiry-into-online-relationships/.
5 Maeve McDermott, "Nicki Minaj's 'Queen': A Track-by-Track Review," *USA Today*, August 10, 2018, accessed September 20, 2021, https://www.usatoday.com/story/life/music/2018/08/10/nicki-minaj-releases-new-album-queen/955722002/.
6 Rudolf Leopold, *Egon Schiele Landscapes* (Munich: Prestel, 2004), 98.
7 See Arnie Cox, *Music and Embodied Cognition: Listening, Moving, Feeling, and Thinking* (Bloomington: Indiana University Press, 2016).
8 Michaeleen Doucleff, "Anatomy of a Tear-Jerker; Why Does Adele's 'Someone Like You' Make Everyone Cry? Science Has Found the Formula," *Wall Street Journal*, February 11, 2012, accessed May 28, 2019, https://ezproxy.hws.edu/login?url=https://search.proquest.com/docview/920884384?accountid=27680.
9 Ibid.

10 Ava Louise, "The Timeless Voice of Billie Holiday," *All About Jazz*, February 6, 2018, accessed June 2, 2020, https://www.allaboutjazz.com/the-timeless-voice-of-billie-holiday-billie-holiday-by-ava-louise.
11 Ibid.
12 Andy Gill, "Billie Holiday Centenary: The Singer Changed the Face of Music But Her Final Recordings Are Painful to Hear," *Independent*, April 17, 2015, accessed August 3, 2022, https://www.independent.co.uk/arts-entertainment/music/features/billie-holiday-centenary-the-singer-changed-the-face-of-music-but-her-final-recordings-are-painful-to-hear-10182524.html.
13 Geoffrey Himes, "What Makes Billie Holiday's Music so Powerful Today," *Smithsonian Magazine*, April 7, 2015, accessed July 1, 2023, https://www.smithsonianmag.com/arts-culture/what-makes-billie-holiday-so-powerful-today-180954893/.
14 Martin Gayford, "It's the Intensity That Counts," *The Telegraph*, March 29, 2004, accessed April 16, 2022, https://www.telegraph.co.uk/culture/music/rockandjazzmusic/3614599/Its-the-intensity-that-counts.html.
15 Jim Samson, "Genre," *Grove Music Online*, 2001, accessed July 30, 2023, https://www-oxfordmusiconline-com.ezproxy.hws.edu/grovemusic/view/10.1093/gmo/9781561592630.001.0001/omo-9781561592630-e-0000040599.
16 Paul Bowers, "Hakon Kornstad Plays Complex One-Man Jazz—with Fits of Opera," *Charleston City Paper*, June 4, 2014, accessed October 21, 2020, https://charlestoncitypaper.com/2014/06/04/hakon-kornstad-plays-complex-one-man-jazz-with-fits-of-opera-2/.
17 Bill Lasarow, "Art Versus Entertainment: The Gap Is Essential," *HuffPost*, ArtScene, July 26, 2010, December 6, 2017, September 20, 2021, https://www.huffpost.com/entry/art-versus-entertainment_b_658792.

# 5 Interpreting Music

In 1909, the French composer, Claude Debussy, published his second book of 12 piano preludes, to include a much-heralded little piece called "Voiles." Borrowing from the visual arts, critics and historians have frequently cast the piece as impressionistic. The term, "impressionism" derives from Monet's eponymous *Impression Sunrise* (Impression, Soleil-Levant), 1872, which exemplifies the use of short, thin brushstrokes and pure, often-unmixed color to capture general impressions, often of natural scenes outdoors, rather than specific and detailed likenesses.

Debussy's active period was a full generation later than Monet's (not to mention, in an entirely different medium); however, the correspondences among his music and the now well-established impressionist style were duly noted by critics and fans. Among the first to use the term impressionism to describe Debussy's music was his friend and biographer, Louis Laloy, who, in 1908, deemed "Reflets dans l'eau" (Reflections in the Water) an "impressionistic sketch" and offered his own programmatic text to accompany the piece: "The rippling flow and trickle of a running stream is heard; the cool, translucent effect and gurgle of disturbed water is given."[1]

Laloy might just as well have had "Voiles" in mind when composing that text, with its watery suggestions of stillness and movement. Watery, indeed. Inspired by the title, "Voiles," which translates to the English word, "sails," the listener imagines herself to be embarking on an impressionistic journey across the sea, where whole tone scales evoking calm waters are disrupted, in the middle section, by pentatonic and chromatic "gusts of wind."

As compelling as this interpretation is, which reflects both the title of the work and the broader Zeitgeist of early 20th French artistic culture, it nevertheless ignores one significant consideration; the French word, "voiles" is a homonym, which means both "sails" and "veils."

This second meaning of the title invites an entirely different interpretation of the piece. Pointing away from painterly scenes or nature, the title, read as "Veils," connects to French literary symbolists operating in Paris in the late nineteenth century.[2] While impressionists were bringing forth a

DOI: 10.4324/9780429505171-8

*Figure 5.1* Claude Monet, *Impression Sunrise*, 1872

"hidden clarity" through their play with light and texture, Symbolist poets drew on synesthesia and representations of the occult. Baudelaire's iconic poem, "Correspondences" offers an exquisite example of the symbolist movement, with its allusions to the infinite, the unknown, and the hidden aspects of human sensory experience:

> *l est des parfums frais comme des chairs d'enfants,*
> *Doux comme les hautbois, verts comme les prairies,*
> *– Et d'autres, corrompus, riches et triomphants,*
>
> *Ayant l'expansion des choses infinies,*
> *Comme l'ambre, le musc, le benjoin et l'encens,*
> *Qui chantent les transports de l'esprit et des sens.*
>
> (There are smells that are fresh like children's skin,
> calm like oboes, green like meadows
> – And others, rotten, heady, and triumphant,
> having the expansiveness of infinite things,
> like amber, musk, benzoin, and incense,
> which sing of the raptures of the soul and senses.)

As "veils," the piece presents a world of mystery; the whole tone scale, which lacks a leading tone, situates the opening music in a directionless realm. The veil lifts briefly in the middle section, only to be replaced as the opening material returns in varied form.[3] Listening to the weightless, ethereal chords and arpeggios in "Voiles," which translation of the title feels more convincing to you? Your answer to this question is the seat of your musical interpretation.

## Musical Interpretation

Musical interpretation refers to the attribution of meaning to a musical work. Whereas description concerns itself with verifiable "facts" and agreed-upon aspects of a work, interpretation uses those facts as building blocks for the construction of meaning. It thus follows that while descriptive features are objectively present or absent, correct or incorrect:

> **There is no such thing as a correct (or incorrect) interpretation. Interpretations are either persuasive or unpersuasive.**

Debussy seems to be making this point in titling his work with a homonym. By offering multiple valid ways to hear the piece, Debussy seems to be arguing for music's interpretive subjectivity. To be sure, some philosophers defend the notion of an ideal interpretation, which communicates the essential truth of the work at hand. Increasingly, however, a defining aspect of interpretation is seen to be "its tolerance of alternative and seemingly contrary hypotheses."[4] Matters such as these belong to the realm of hermeneutics: the branch of knowledge dealing with interpretation and meaning. Hermeneutics concerns itself with broad questions such as, *What is the purpose of interpretation? Is there a single right interpretation?* However you answer these questions, it must be acknowledged that any critical interpretation is a hypothesis, which goes beyond the literal, observable, objective understanding of the piece to reveal a dialogue between the interpreter and the work. Whether you hear the unfolding music in "Voiles" as mysterious or bucolic will depend in part on your own listening habits, experiences, and personality. In this sense,

> **The interpreter is always part and parcel of the interpretation.**

Surely, though, the author is the ultimate arbiter of interpretive meaning, right? Not always. Consider the controversial 2013 song, "Blurred Lines." The popular song spent 12 weeks on the top of the Billboard Hot 100, was certified Diamond by the Record Industry Association of America, and was nominated for two Grammys that year. Nevertheless, shortly after its release, controversy ensued over the lyrics, which seem to endorse blurring the lines of sexual consent. Thicke himself described these controversial lyrics as a feminist testament to women's inherent (but repressed) sexual energy and the blurred lines between a "good girl" and a "bad girl." Elsewhere he added that the song is about his wife.[5]

Reviewing the lyrics, it is easy to see why Thicke's interpretation was widely considered unpersuasive. Implications that a man knows what a woman wants (without her communicating it directly) are not easily reconciled with notions of female empowerment and marital love. Furthermore, "Blurred Lines" was released during the #MeToo movement, which led to heightened awareness of and responsiveness to sexist, patriarchal, and abusive messaging. Most music critics interpreted the song in opposition to Thicke's explanation. Here's a biting review of the song, published in 2019 in the *New Statesman*:

> Once upon a time, a pop song was released. The pop song told us that sexual consent is a grey area. It suggested that women were "bitches" and "animals", and something a man could "take". It had a popular music video featuring three slim, topless female models, dancing playfully around two suited men, who sing "I know you want it" as the models wink, giggle and toss their hair. It was number one in the UK for five weeks in a row.
> [. . .]
> Of course, at the time, Pharrell and many others claimed not to understand why the song caused such controversy. . . . Pharell himself told Pitchfork that critics of the video "just want to be mad".[6]

"Blurred Lines" is a controversial example of a more neutral philosophical problem of authorial intention. William Wimsatt, Jr. and Monroe Beardsley's seminal essay, "The Intentional Fallacy" takes the position that a creator simply cannot control the meanings ascribed to a work upon its release.[7] For Wimsatt and Beardsley, a work's meaning is determined by a composite of historical, cultural, and artistic factors that transcend author's intention. The "Blurred Lines" example seems to prove their point:

**Even the author/artist cannot fully control the meanings ascribed to a work.**

This is not to say that a composer's intentions or experiences do not inform a work or an interpretation. In fact, an entire school of criticism, biographical criticism, rests on perceived connections between a work and its creator. For example, critics have long ascribed autobiographical meanings to Beethoven's *Eroica* symphony, despite that it was originally dedicated to Napoleon Bonaparte; and Berlioz's *Symphonie Fantastique* resonates for critics and historians with the composer's real-life fascination with the actor, Harriet Smithson.

Nevertheless, it is the listener, not the artist, who ultimately determines a work's meaning, as Berlioz (like Beethoven before him) expressed no wish for the piece to be interpreted as it was.

90  *Criticizing Music*

*Figure 5.2* Harriett Smithson Portrait, George Clint, c. 1850

**What a work means may not be what it meant.**

A well-known example of the influence of time on a work's meaning is the 1944 hit, "Baby its Cold Outside," written by Frank Loesser and featured in the 1949 film, *Neptune's Daughter*. The song won an Academy Award in 1950, was covered by dozens of popular artists, became a mainstay of the holiday season, and was named by *Time Magazine* as one of the 100 Best Songs of All Time. Nevertheless, controversy over the lyrics has mounted over the years; the lyrics, like those in "Blurred Lines," seem to suggest that sexual consent is implied and pursued, rather than offered. The song is a duet, featuring a dialogue between a man, who is encouraging his date to stay at his house, and the date, who offers reasons to leave.

There's no question that certain phrases, such as one in which she questions what's in her drink, undermine a woman's right to say no to sexual advances. How could such a song possibly have become a hit? In order to answer this question, one has to consider the culture of American sexual politics in the 1950s. Whereas today, a primary concern of feminism is women's right to say no to sexual advances, in the 1950s, there were also repressive restrictions on a woman's right to say yes. According to Alfred Kinsey's groundbreaking *Sexual Behavior in Human Male*, (1948), about half of American men in the midcentury wanted to marry a virgin; more than 60% of college-educated men and 80% of college-educated women said they disapproved of premarital sex; abortion was federally criminalized, contraception was illegal in most states, and unwed pregnant women could lawfully be kicked out of school or home and forced to give their baby up for adoption. Women could in fact be incarcerated for being promiscuous.

Whereas today the song reads as an ironic commentary on a woman's right to say no to sexual advances; it may have read in the 1950s as a commentary on the external pressure to say no and the unfairness of the standard courtship ritual. Lines expressing concern that friends and family will be suspicious if she stays speak indeed to these external pressures.

For these reasons, some critics have gone so far as to defend the song as essentially feminist in its outlook. Consider this review published in *Variety* in 2018:

> "Baby, It's Cold Outside" is the story of a woman doing battle—not with a guy who won't take no for an answer, but with the expectations of a society that won't take yes for an answer. The most critical word in the whole piece is "ought," as in, "I ought to say no, no, no sir." She isn't trying to fend off advances—she is mouthing excuses so she can "at least . . . *say* that I tried." He won't face judgment sneaking home, whereas she can tick off at least three family members who'll notice when she sneaks in after hours. It's not just the kinfolk but a nation of suspicious minds there at the door, waiting to sniff the cigarettes, booze and boys on her breath. At least two out of three of which she is explicitly the one asking for, by the way: "maybe just a cigarette more," she requests, along with "maybe just half a drink more." She is not being plied with alcohol—she is plying herself, with intoxicating stalling tactics she hopes will make the "spell" of romance and sexual chemistry finally out-loom the specter of the family scowling behind the porch light.

> The fellow in the song makes some pretty funny arguments, including the threat of pneumonia, a rationale maybe even the vicious aunt would find acceptable for a couch sleepover. But he's really the secondary character in the song. It's not about acceding to a dangerous wolf. It's about her succumbing to her own she-wolf. Which, at the very end, she does, taking part in the closing bit of harmony and agreeing: As a matter of fact, dude, I *will* catch my death of cold out there.[8]

Others have taken a less direct tact in responding to controversy over its meaning and implications. One year after the *Variety* review, John Legend and Kelly Clarkson released a remake of "Baby It's Cold Outside"; one that reimagines the scene for a #MeToo sensitive audience with lines about calling her a cab and respecting her body and her choices.

In general, the remake has been well received. A *Vanity Fair* profile of Legend and his wife noted that "The song's every bit as fun and swinging as the original, and its newfound sensitivity feels genuine, not performative";[9] others, though, still defend the original as misunderstood, arguing that time and cultural conditions have shaped the current (mis-) understanding of the lyrics. In the meantime, the song remains a prominent feature of the holiday canon, for reasons that may transcend the controversy.

**Not all meaning is narrative or pictorial, as not all music tells a story or depicts an image.**

Some art simply doesn't have a story to tell. Consider Pollock's drip paintings. Critics tend not to search for representations of autumn in the work precisely because representational features are denied. "Autumn" for example is widely seen as a painting about paint and painting.

> Each line records a gesture, and as such inscribes the act and process of painting. Moreover, the paint is not a vehicle for the depiction of something else but rather made to reveal paint as paint—pooling and dripping and sliding across the canvas.

For some music critics and philosophers, similarly, music is to be understood as providing an experience that needs no elucidation. For Eduard Hanslick, famously,

> What kind of beauty is the beauty of a musical composition? It is a specifically musical kind of beauty. By this we understand a beauty that is self-contained and in no need of content from outside itself, that consists simply and solely of tones and their artistic combination . . . . It is

# Interpreting Music 93

an end in itself, and it is in no way primarily a medium or material for the representation of feelings or conceptions.[10]

For Hanslick, music is an end rather than a means, and its meaning is no more or less than the beauty it contains.
Even when a work does have a story to tell and an essence to parse or decipher,

**The matter of a work's essential meaning is only one of a number of questions that an interpretation might answer.**

Returning to Debussy's "Voiles," beyond the meaning of the piece, one might ask, How does this piece reflect the emotional tenor of war-era France? How is "Voiles" a product of Debussy's musical training? What is the significance of the location of this piece in the larger set? Could

*Figure 5.3* Piet Mondrian, Rasterkombination 8- Schachbrettkomposition mit dunklen Farben (Composition with Grid 8- Checkerboard Composition with Dark Colors), 1919

"Voiles" mean both "Sails" and "Veils"? In what ways does "Voiles" employ a white male musical lexicon? Each of these questions situates the facts of the work in a subjective context. In this essay by Gerald Larner for the BBC Music Magazine, the question of "Voiles" double meaning is expediently dismissed as the author takes up the alternative issue of the impact and meaning of Debussy's tonal language:

> What Debussy was doing in the *Préludes* and earlier works with a similar inspiration was composing with sounds rather than notes . . . . Debussy did nothing less than liberate music from the domination by functional harmony which had prevailed for three centuries. Take "Voiles" from *Préludes* Book I: whether it was intended to create an impression of "veils" or "sails" (the French title could refer to either) it does so by almost exclusive use of the whole-tone and pentatonic scales. That doesn't make it strictly atonal but it does set it free from the triad to float wherever the movement of the dancer or the wind on the water takes it.[11]

This claim that, in "Voiles," tonality becomes color is an interpretive one, which, rather than parsing out the meaning of the work, situates it within the broader history of tonality. For Larner, Debussy's *Preludes* presaged (and informed) Schönberg's "emancipation of tonality," thus changing the course of music history. In this sense, Larner is concerned less with the piece's story or narrative than with its technical musical features:

## Interpretive Strategies

We have thus far focused largely on titles and text-music relationships in examining musical interpretations. However, interpretations may arise from many considerations, including

- The relationship of the work to its genre or category
- The relationship of the work to the broader cultural and/or political arena
- The composer's previous work
- The composer's life experience
- The text and text-music relationships
- Expressive features of the music
- Intertextual features of the text and/or music
- Innovations and unusual features of the music

All of these considerations bear out in Alexis Petridis's review of Taylor Swift's 2019 album, *Lover*. The author begins by relating the album to

Swift's previous work, focusing specifically on her *Reputation* album, "a messy, uneven explosion of bitterness and cynicism amid the love songs, on which Swift's desire for public redress sometimes overwhelmed her songwriting smarts."[12] He then turns to her own life experience and the diaristic tone of the album:

> The tone of Lover is noticeably different from its predecessor, the bitterness largely expunged in favour of besotted paeans to her British partner, actor Joe Alwyn. He gets hymned in every conceivable way, from the Mazzy Star-ish title track to London Boy.[13]

The author next probes the album's relationship to Swift's commercial audience and the place of the work in its genre category before exploring, in greater detail, expressive features of the music:

> That said, Lover's highlights come when Swift ignores the outside world, whether that's politics, public image or the desire to reassert her pop dominance . . . .They hint at another album, buried amid Lover's landslide of styles and lyrical approaches, more subtle and low-key and experimental, but potentially more satisfying.[14]

Ultimately, the meaning that this critic deems most prominent is the commercial "something for everyone" quality of the music, which is nevertheless set against her strong songwriting skills, diaristic writing style, and tremendous fame:

> As it is, Lover offers plenty of evidence that Swift is just a better songwriter than any of her competitors in the upper echelons of pop, but its something-for-everyone approach feels like consolidation, not progress, designed to keep Swift as one of the world's biggest stars without provoking the kind of backlash that led her to start evoking the end of days in her diary.[15]

Whether or not you are persuaded by this author's interpretation, it employs multiple intersecting strategies to make meaning out of the work.

## Chapter Summary

This chapter invites the reader to explore the meaning and purpose of a given musical work and offers guiding principles of musical interpretation. Interpretations emerge from within the sounding music (and text, if there is one), from contexts outside of the music, or from a combination of the two. The main points of the chapter are as follows:

- There is no such thing as a correct interpretation of a musical work; interpretations are either persuasive or unpersuasive.
- The author's intentions may or may not inform a critic's interpretation. This is articulated in Monroe Beardsley's notion of "The Intentional Fallacy."
- Interpretations arise from considerations such as the following:
  - The relationship of the work to its genre or category
  - The relationship of the work to the broader cultural and/or political arena
  - The composer's previous work
  - The composer's life experience
  - The text and text-music relationships
  - Expressive features of the music
  - Intertextual features of the text and/or music
  - Innovations and unusual features of the music

## Guide Questions

1. Which meaning of "Voiles" is more convincing to you? Defend your answer.
2. Do you agree with Wimsatt and Beardsley that authorial intention does not dictate the meaning of the work? Can you think of an example that contradicts their thesis? What about one that supports it?
3. Should we apply historical values and perspectives to historical music (like "Baby, It's Cold Outside"), or should we engage with it from a contemporary perspective? Justify your response.
4. Think of an example where an artist's life experience informed a particular song or album. How does that information influence the listening experience?
5. Do you agree with the critic's review of Taylor Swift, *Lover*, above? The author of the essay takes a particular perspective on the work. What other perspective might he have taken? Would it have led to alternative conclusions?

## Notes

1 See Eric Frederick Jensen, *Debussy* (Oxford: Oxford University Press, 2014), 123.
2 Richard Taruskin, *Music in the Early Twentieth Century: The Oxford History of Twentieth Century Music* (New York: Oxford University Press, 2009), 83–89.
3 Ibid.
4 John F. Reichert, "Description and Interpretation in Literary Criticism," *The Journal of Aesthetics and Art Criticism* 27, no. 3 (1969): 281–292, https://doi.org/10.2307/428674.

5 Nesta McGregor and Jimmy Blake, "Robin Thicke: I Don't Think People Got Blurred Lines," *BBC News*, October 10, 2013, accessed March 20, 2022, https://www.bbc.com/news/newsbeat-24471006.
6 Emily Bootle, "How the Blurred Lines Scandal Changed Pop," *The New Statesman*, October 17, 2019, November 20, 2022, https://www.newstatesman.com/culture/music/2019/10/blurred-lines-scandal-changed-pop-controversial.
7 W. K. Wimsatt Jr. and M. C. Beardsley, "The Intentional Fallacy," *The Sewanee Review* 54, no. 3 (July–September 1947): 468–488.
8 Chris Willman, "End the War on 'Baby, It's Cold Outside'! It's Feminist—Really," *Variety*, December 5, 2018, accessed May 22, 2022, https://variety.com/2018/music/news/baby-its-cold-outside-song-war-1203080834/.
9 Karen Valby, "John Legend and Chrissy Teigen on Love, Childhood Traumas, and the 'Sh—ty Human Being' in the White House," *Vanity Fair*, December 2019, accessed July 13, 2023, https://www.vanityfair.com/hollywood/2019/10/john-legend-and-chrissy-teigen-cover-story.
10 Eduard Hanslick, *On the Musically Beautiful*, trans. Geoffrey Payzant (Indianapolis, IN: Hackett, 1986), 28.
11 Gerald Larner, "The Story of Debussy's Préludes (1909–1913)," *BBC Music Magazine*, August 19, 2016, accessed July 14, 2023, https://www.classical-music.com/articles/story-debussy-s-pr-ludes-1909-13.
12 Alexis Petridis, "Taylor Swift: Lover Review—Pop Denominator Wears Her Heart on Her Sleeve," *The Guardian*, August 23, 2019, accessed September 21, 2023, https://www.theguardian.com/music/2019/aug/23/taylor-swift-lover-review.
13 Ibid.
14 Ibid.
15 Ibid.

# 6 Evaluating Music

### Some Negative Criticism of Negative Criticism

When we think of critical evaluations, we often think of negative reviews, such as this one of Andrew Lloyd Weber's last and latest musical, *Bad Cinderella*; here the critic recommends bringing earplugs, eye plugs, and, if you can find them, soul plugs:

> That's because "Bad Cinderella" is not the clever, high-spirited revamp you might have expected, casting contemporary fairy dust on the classic story of love and slippers . . . . Instead, it's surprisingly vulgar, sexed-up and dumbed-down: a parade of hustling women in bustiers and shirtless pec-rippling hunks.[1]

If this review seems to amount to mean-spirited moralizing, this critic at least justifies their evaluation by pointing to discernible features of the music and performance. For this critic, the bombast and excess of the music, costumes, and staging are a mismatch with the "flippant" fairytale, which, for them, requires a lighter touch. This critic observes a copy-paste strategy from the excesses of *Phantom of the Opera*, also by Lloyd Weber, but remarks that *Phantom* was an opera about obsession, and so the performative excess was mirrored by the story; in this one, not so much:

> *Phantom* was a show about obsession, so its richness and hysteria made sense. If anything, Bad Cinderella is about plotting how to "marry for love" (the title of a song in the second act) and thus requires a much lighter touch.[2]

For this critic, *Bad Cinderella*'s aggressively bombastic setting is irreconcilable with the ever-delicate fairytale. Though this evaluation is justified, it is perhaps still not just. Indeed, the critic must acknowledge that *Bad*

DOI: 10.4324/9780429505171-9

*Cinderella's* creator, the inimitable Andrew Lloyd Weber, has defied critics' snubs at the box office for thirty-five years:

> Lloyd Webber, not only British but a Lord, has been, in that sense, America's most successful theater composer. We can argue that "Evita" wasn't good for the culture—and "Cats" not good for anything—but somehow, he and Broadway made a match that's lasted like no other. Even without the blessing of critics, and just like "Bad Cinderella," it's an implausible story about a real marriage of love.[3]

Here is where this negative criticism must earn some negative criticism of its own: at its best, critics are mediators between art and the public; they assist audiences in identifying what, in a work, is worthy of contemplation, inquiry, and experience. Whereas this review does little more than hold its nose against the gaudy and strident performance, effective evaluations are fundamentally constructive and supportive of the artform and its practitioners.

This is not to say that there's no place for negative reviews. Nevertheless, behind every creation is a (group of) creators, whose efforts inevitably involve risk and vulnerability. To criticize a work without demoralizing the creator(s) requires wisdom, clarity, and skill. Effective criticism avoids mean-spirited click-bait messaging and aims instead to be honest, constructive, and respectful.

A more pointed and effective—though ultimately also negative—response to Lloyd Weber's *Bad Cinderella* was published around the same time in *Entertainment Weekly*.[4] The review begins by acknowledging the talent and achievements of the work's creators and pointing to its many impressive attributes, including performances by "the Queen and the wicked Stepmother (Carolee Carmello) who are the true rulers of Bad Cinderella and, honestly, long may they reign." The reviewer also commends the show's set design and lighting, which "evokes a dreamy atmosphere with a sky full of shimmering stars."[5]

In addressing the negative aspects of the work, this critic brings to light features that are perceivable when uncovered but not immediately obvious to the casual observer. Whereas a philistine can make note of the bombast that was the focus of the first review, the second reviewer's emphasis on the messaging brings to light new and deeper miscarriages in the work:

> Though she appears confident and unapologetic in song, Cinderella is strangely passive and has little to no sense of personal agency throughout the show.... The only thing that feels concrete is her staunch rejection of the town's beauty standards, which is why it is both jarring and

confusing when she later decides to transform into a pretty princess in order to vie for Sebastian's affections—especially given that he's praised her eccentricities beforehand.[6]

Perhaps most importantly, this review emphasizes confusion around the messaging. This work's fatal flaw, we learn, is that its purpose and meaning are muddled; rather than snubbing a "hilariously campy romp," this reviewer focuses on the lack of clear identity, thus reorienting criticism from personal (and often classist) judgment to the more fruitful question of the purpose of the work:

> Herein lies *Bad Cinderella*'s biggest problem: like its protagonists, it doesn't know what it wants to be. At times, it's an ominous cautionary tale of how the beauty industry—led by the Fairy Godmother (Christina Acosta Robinson), who excitedly waves a syringe instead of a wand—preys on insecurities and coerces others to conform to its unrealistic standards. At others, it's a critique on how fairytale endings don't actually exist, only for the show to culminate in its own highly dramatic happily ever after. And, at its best, it's a hilariously campy romp that doesn't take itself seriously in the slightest.[7]

### Evaluation and the Work's Purpose

As repeatedly discussed, art is subjective, so evaluations are necessarily subjective as well. To be sure, critics validate their evaluations by becoming experts in their subject matter; beyond this, however, critics don't necessarily have firsthand experience of artistic creation; they aren't necessarily artists themselves. Criticism isn't about evaluating artistic process; that is the purview of the artist. Criticism is about evaluating the effect. In other words, the evaluation answers the question, "Did the work achieve its intended effect? Did it satisfy its purpose?" The second *Bad Cinderella* review does a better job of making space for multiple, equally valid types of purpose, and the reviewer's ultimately negative evaluation is focused not on the value of a presumed purpose but on the lack of clarity as to what the purpose or meaning is. Is it an "ominous cautionary tale," a "critique of fairytale endings," or a "hilariously campy romp"? The work waffles among these different storylines without settling convincingly on any one of them.

> **The successful critic begins with the question, "What is the purpose of the work"?**

For the answer to this question, the successful critic turns primarily to the genre, sentiment, expression, context, and audience:

## Genre

Genre provides an excellent starting point for evaluating a work's purpose. As articulated elsewhere in this book, Adele's rich, raspy tone might be unwelcome in the world of opera; however, as a soul singer, her voice is one of her strongest attributes. A long, searching guitar solo would be out of place in most commercial rap songs, but it is an essential feature of much classic rock. Locating a work within its genre category provides an important context for evaluating its purpose and value.

## Sentiment

Sentiment concerns the disposition of the work and the perspective that it takes on the subject. Consider, for example, love songs; this genre encompasses a variety of different attitudes about and perspectives on love. One love song might be a celebration of true love, whereas another might present love as a source of suffering. One need only compare Joan Jett's "I Hate Myself for Loving You" with Billy Joel's "Just the Way You Are" to understand the importance of considering sentiment in evaluating a work's meaning and purpose.

## Expression

If the sentiment of the work represents its attitude, the expression is the voice of that attitude. Indeed, Joan Jett's up-tempo, guitar-heavy, rock anthem expresses a different sentiment from the soft-rock crooning, set against the saxophone and Fender Rhodes, featured in the Billy Joel song. Each song uses expressive resources to convey a particular sentiment or attitude about the subject matter. The critic may consider the elements of music discussed in Chapter 4 in determining a work's expression and relating that to its sentiment and purpose.

## Context

A work's purpose is also tied to its performance context. A live album will have a decidedly different sound quality and character than a studio album, which is created in a controlled environment with isolated tracks and numerous takes. By contrast, a live album seeks to transmit some of the energy and ephemerality of the live experience, while forfeiting the control and intentionality that characterizes the studio album. In the realm of classical music, outdoor concerts like those performed by the Boston Symphony Orchestra at Tanglewood each summer will have markedly different acoustics from those in the symphony hall in Boston. To consider a work's purpose without engaging with the performance context misses an opportunity for a fuller engagement with its meaning.

### Audience

Finally, one should consider the audience in determining a work's purpose. Is there a language barrier between the music and the audience? Demographic characteristics, including age, gender identity, and ethnicity can influence an audience's expectations and experiences. Identity politics can also influence an audience's response to the music they're consuming. For example, female folk duo, *The Chicks*, changed their name from *The Dixie Chicks* when the racist connotations of the term Dixie entered mainstream discourse. Understanding the audience for a work provides essential information about its purpose.

These are some of the primary resources that a critic may use in answering the question, "Does the work achieve its purpose?" Following this question is another, perhaps thornier, one: "What is the value of the work's purpose?" This is an equally important question to ask, given that evaluation is ultimately about value.

**It is incumbent on the critic to consider not only the work's fittedness to its purpose but also the value of that purpose.**

There are different types of purpose and, with them, value. Consider, for example, Mozart's Andante for mechanical organ clock, K. 616; this diminutive little piece was commissioned by Count Joseph Deym for his eclectic museum containing plaster casts of ancient statues, wax figures of famous people, mechanical instruments, including an automatic piano, musical pyramid, a mechanical (singing) canary, and flute-playing Spanish children. Mozart's associations with this shop and its proprietor were born of financial need. In a letter to his wife during the composition of this work, he remarked dryly:

> I have now made up my mind to compose at once the Adagio for the clockmaker and then to slip a few ducats into the hand of my dear little wife; and this I have done—but as it is the very kind of work which I detest, I have unfortunately not been able to finish it—I compose a bit of it every day—but I have to break off now and then, as I get bored. And indeed I would give the whole thing up, if I had not such an important reason to go on with it. But I still hope that I shall be able to force myself gradually to finish it.[8]

Evaluating Music 103

This static, repetitious little piece, which was inscribed mechanically into a small table-top organ clock (not unlike a music box) indeed serves its purpose; its purpose, however, was to satisfy the caprice of an aberrant collector for financial gain. To evaluate the work only on the satisfaction of its intended purpose misses an important aspect of the work's value, which is somewhat diminished by the need that engendered its creation.

*Figure 6.1* German organ clock, c. 1625

## The Value of the Purpose

To consider the value of a work's purpose, one may engage with the work's aesthetic, cultural, moral, intellectual, entertainment, and/or commercial meanings. Each one is briefly discussed below:

### Aesthetic Value

As discussed in previous chapters, aesthetics refers to a category of experience in which disinterested pleasure results from perceiving something in the environment. Nature provides myriad opportunities for this experience: shooting stars, sunsets, mountain ranges, and flowers all provide opportunities to derive pleasure from the pure experience of nature's canvas. Human-made art similarly provides opportunities for disinterested pleasure. It should be noted, however, that aesthetics is an expansive realm, and aesthetic pleasure is not derived solely from the experience of beauty. Some people derive tremendous pleasure from horror movies; some like music with a lot of distortion and dissonance. Aesthetic value is determined by the pleasure derived from a (any) compelling artistic experience, which may just as well be offered by *Epica*, the female-fronted Dutch metal band as by the music of J.S. Bach.

### Cultural Value

Music plays an important role in the gatherings, rituals, and celebrations that form and reinforce culture. Music is often incorporated in such events, including weddings, funerals, graduation ceremonies, religious and spiritual events, reunions, and other moments of importance and recognition. In this sense, it can be a way of recording collective memories and sharing knowledge. Sometimes music forfeits some of its aesthetic or entertainment value for its ceremonial or ritual-cultural value. For example, the first thousand years of sacred music in the Roman Catholic church comprised unaccompanied singing. Instruments (with the exception of the organ) were not used in liturgical music because they were seen to distract from music's essential purpose, which was to connect the listener to God and to heighten their devotion and faith. In this case, the cultural and spiritual value of the music superseded the aesthetic value; considering value from this alternate perspective offers an important perspective on the music.

### Moral Value

Sometimes the purpose of music is to advance or communicate a social justice message. In the 1960s in the United States, civil rights activists repurposed African American Spirituals—a category of sacred folk song created by enslaved people in the United States—to protest for equal rights for people of color and other disenfranchised groups. In some cases, melodies were retained from the original spirituals, while the texts were updated to meet the moment. For example, the spiritual, "Woke Up This Morning with My Mind Stayed on Jesus," was repurposed to state the word "freedom" in place of the word "Jesus." In this case, the Freedom song was layered on the spiritual so that the power and significance of the original song carried through to the new context. The songs themselves often followed a simple repetition structure suitable for acapella singing in a group setting. These features served the moral and political functions of the music.

*Intellectual Value*

In 1958, an essay by the composer Milton Babbitt was published in a prominent journal with the title, "Who Cares if You Listen."[9] In the essay, Babbitt argues that composers should relinquish their allegiance to the general public in the service of advancing the art and science of music. For Babbitt, music should be approached like any other academic pursuit; that is, systematically by trained experts. Few of us take such an extreme view of music's intellectualism, but there are times when music's primary value is intellectual. Leroy Anderson's infamous Typewriter song, *Ritvélin*, is best understood as a commentary on the fine line between music and noise; John Cage's 4'33", which prescribes four minutes, thirty-three seconds of relative silence, similarly communicates an appreciation for the music that is all around us, in the sounds of a person shuffling in their seat, unwrapping a cough drop or clearing their throat. To evaluate these works on their aesthetic value alone may leave the question of meaning un- or underexamined.

*Entertainment Value*

Perhaps the greatest quantity of music in the public sphere foregrounds its entertainment value. Returning to the two reviews of *Bad Cinderella*, the first reviewer, in acknowledging the discrepancy between critics' responses to Lloyd Weber's musicals and their showings at the box office, points to an analogous discrepancy in how value is attributed. Reviewer one seems to dismiss out of hand the entertainment value of the work, which justifies the consistent box office returns. Instead, the reviewer focuses on the work's effect on the ears, eyes, and soul—in other words, this reviewer uses aesthetic and moral measures to evaluate the work, whose fundamental purpose seems to have been to entertain.

*Commercial Value*

Entertainment value is often tied to commercial value, which concerns the profitability of a musical artifact. To be sure, commercial interests can frustrate and sometimes even contradict other values, as argued in relation to the Mozart organ clock piece, K. 616, discussed above. However, the public often uses commercial success as a shorthand for determining value. Many readers consult *The New York Times* Bestseller List to determine what to read, although the list is constructed solely on weekly sales reports from bookstores (and wholesalers) across the United States. In music, the Recording Industry Association of America (RIAA) awards albums the coveted statuses of gold, platinum, and multiplatinum based on sales. These awards, in turn, confer a certain prestige on the album and its creators, which often translates to more sales. As these examples suggest, the consumer marketplace seems to provide its own valuation, which may seem to obviate critical ones. This, however, is a shortsighted view, as what is most popular is not always what has the most value. Thus, as literary critic Noël Carroll writes, "the education of the audience, it must be said, is the critic's primary brief."[10]

### The Critic as Educator

For Carroll, "assisting audiences in apprehending and understanding what is valuable in the work at hand is the primary function of the critic and her critical work."[11]

> The best criticism, then, focuses on what is worthy of contemplation, inquiry, and/or experience,

independent of the commercial sphere. At its best, compelling, insightful criticism can enhance consumer interest in a musical work or album and ultimately boost sales; however, the two spheres—the commercial sphere and the critical one—should not be confused for one and the same.

*Pitchfork Review* is known for engaging with lesser-known artists and albums and, as such, has many times launched a band out of obscurity with a positive review. So common is this occurrence that the industry widely calls it the "Pitchfork Effect." To be sure, *Pitchfork* and other prominent publications have damaged careers as well; however, as discussed above, there is limited value to publishing negative reviews:

> **Selection is its own type of evaluation.**

Critics (theoretically) choose what to highlight, discuss, and draw attention to; and negative reviews should be approached sparingly, carefully, and respectfully. I love the bait and switch style of this review of the New Bloods' album, *The Secret Life*, which begins by discussing all of the features of the music that shouldn't, but somehow do, work:

> On paper, the New Bloods' disparate musical styles don't sound like such a great combo: . . . [contrasting] angular and aggressive rhythmic

bass and drum attacks with a joyously twisted Americana violin— . . . velvety smooth vocal lines, . . . sing-song-y speak-sing, and . . . sporadic reggae-toasting shouts. It shouldn't work, but it does. It's a wild and wonderful combination where weird individual parts coalesce to make a unified songwriting machine.[12]

Nevertheless, selection does not in itself mean privileging. As Carroll argues, historians select negative events for scrutiny all the time. The Holocaust is considered worthy of study, not because of any positive valence ascribed to this historical event, but rather because of its significance. Similarly, songs like "Blurred Lines" and "Baby It's Cold Outside," discussed in the previous chapter, call out for negative scrutiny. So negative criticism does occur, but not for the sole purpose of discouraging or disparaging; the educational, didactic, or moral value of the negative criticism should justify its publication.

**Time sometimes proves evaluations wrong.**

What does it mean to say that a critic "got it all wrong"? After all, criticism isn't a factual domain of correct and incorrect answers; it's the realm of taste and opinion. And yet, we've all heard of infamous critical errors, such as this one, which John Mendelsohn made in writing for *Rolling Stone* magazine in March 1969:

> Jimmy Page, around whom the Zeppelin revolves, is, admittedly, an extraordinarily proficient blues guitarist and explorer of his instrument's electronic capabilities. Unfortunately, he is also a very limited producer and a writer of weak, unimaginative songs, and the Zeppelin album suffers from his having both produced it and written most of it (alone or in combination with his accomplices in the group).[13]

Those "weak," "unimaginative" songs filled an album that went eight times platinum in the United States; reached the top ten on the US, UK, Spanish, Danish, Australian, Polish and Finish charts; and ranks among the *Times* best albums of all time; albums that changed music; greatest debut albums; albums you must hear before you die, and, ironically, *The Rolling Stone* 500 Greatest Albums of All Time. Nonetheless, Mendelsohn is in good company in misreading the impact of an iconic work. In 1970, Lester Bang, writing for *Rolling Stone* magazine, described Black Sabbath's eponymous album:

> a shuck—despite the murky song titles and some inane lyrics that sound like Vanilla Fudge paying doggerel tribute to Aleister Crowley, the album has nothing to do with spiritualism, the occult, or anything

much except stiff recitations of Cream clichés that sound like the musicians learned them out of a book, grinding on and on with dogged persistence.[14]

Robert Christgau referred to Radiohead's masterpiece, *OK Computer*, as "dud of the month" and declared that "Radiohead wouldn't know a tragic hero if they were cramming for their A levels, and their idea of soul is Bono, who they imitate further at the risk of looking even more ridiculous than they already do."[15] Gordon Fletcher, another established critic, hoped, after listening to Brian Eno's release, *Here Come the Warm Jets*, that others would "join [him] in taking exception to this insane divergence of styles and wish that the next time Eno makes an album, he will attempt to structure his work rather than throw together the first ten things that come to mind."[16] The examples go on and on; The National, Lou Reed, Weezer, The Rolling Stones, all received negative reviews by prominent critics upon their most iconic albums' releases. Time proved those critics wrong and became the ultimate arbiter of musical value.

**Chapter Summary**

This chapter engages the theory and practice of evaluating musical works of all kinds. Following Noël Carroll's argument in *On Criticism*, evaluations are made based on how well a piece of music achieves its purpose (or reason for being), and how noble, valuable or relevant that purpose is. The main points of the chapter are as follows:

- For Noël Carroll, evaluation is an essential feature of criticism.
- Positive criticism is generally more valuable than negative criticism.
- Critical evaluations should identify the purpose of the work:
  - Genre
  - Expression
  - Sentiment
  - Audience
- Critical evaluations should articulate the degree to which the work achieves its purpose.
- Critical evaluations should articulate the value of the work's purpose:
  - Aesthetic value
  - Cultural value
  - Moral value
  - Intellectual value
  - Entertainment value
  - Commercial value

## Guide Questions

1. Is there ever a place for negative criticism?
2. Which types of value discussed in this chapter do you find most worthy or most unworthy? Justify your answer.
3. Why can't the commercial value of a work (always) stand in for its aesthetic value?
4. What does it mean to suggest that "selection is its own type of evaluation"?
5. Search magazines, blogs, and other sites to locate a negative review. Does the educational value of the review justify the negative criticism? Why or why not?

## Notes

1 Jesse Green, "Bad Cinderella Review: The Title Warned Us," *The New York Times*, March 24, 2023, accessed May 22, 2023, https://www.nytimes.com/2023/03/24/theater/bad-cinderella-review-broadway.html.
2 Ibid.
3 Ibid.
4 Emlyn Travis, "*Bad Cinderella* Review: Andrew Lloyd Weber's New Musical Is Bibbidi Bobbidi Basic," *Entertainment Weekly*, March 24, 2023, accessed August 1, 2023, https://ew.com/theater/theater-reviews/bad-cinderella-review-andrew-lloyd-webber-musical/.
5 Ibid.
6 Ibid.
7 Ibid.
8 Joseph Eibl, Wilhelm Bauer, Otto Erich Deutsh, and Ulrich Konrad, eds., *Mozart, Briefe und Aufzeichnungen* (Kassel: Bärenreiter, 2005), 4:115; trans., Anderson, *Letters*, 944.
9 Milton Babbitt, "Who Cares If You Listen?" *High Fidelity*, February 1958.
10 Carroll, *On Criticism*, 22.
11 Ibid., 45.
12 Shawn Bosler, "New Bloods *Secret Life* Review," *Pitchfork*, May 1, 2008, accessed September 14, 2023, https://pitchfork.com/reviews/albums/11413-the-secret-life/.
13 John Mendelsohn, "Les Zeppelin I," *Rolling Stone Magazine*, March 15, 1969.
14 Lester Bangs, "Black Sabbath," *Rolling Stone Magazine*, September 17, 1970.
15 Robert Christgau, "Radiohead (1997): Dud of the Month," *The Village Voice*, September 23, 1997.
16 Gordon Fletcher, "Here Come the Warm Jets," *Rolling Stone Magazine*, October 24, 1974.

# Part 3
# Critical Lenses

# 7 Feminist Music Criticism

*Do women have to be naked to get into the Met. Museum?* This question was first raised in the 1980s by a group of feminist activists known as the Guerrilla Girls (who maintain anonymity by wearing gorilla masks when in public) in observing the striking discrepancy between the number of female artists whose work was presented at the Metropolitan Museum of Art in New York and the number of naked female bodies featured in the artworks on display. The slogan was to be presented on a billboard commissioned—but ultimately rejected—by the Public Art Fund in New York in 1989. Ultimately, the campaign was featured on NYC buses and became an iconic symbol of feminist criticism and enduring sexism in the art world.

The Guerrilla Girls are critics in the literal sense—of patriarchy, sexism, and disparate experiences and expectations for women and men—and in the professional sense in that they analyze, interpret, and evaluate cultural artifacts. They do so with a particular lens that informs their interpretations. The lens, as the poster clearly exhibits, is a feminist one.

## Feminism and Feminisms

The word *feminism* originates from Old French *feminina*, meaning *woman*, and *ism*, meaning a doctrine or ideology. This seems to imply that feminism is about privileging and prioritizing women over men. In practice, feminism centers on the pursuit of equality for women in a patriarchal society that advantages men. This unified pursuit notwithstanding, feminism encompasses diverse movements and ideologies that participate in the ongoing fight for political, economic, personal, legal, and social equality of the sexes. Indeed, the plural feminisms may more aptly capture this multi-faceted and even internally conflicted set of beliefs and practices.

DOI: 10.4324/9780429505171-11

*Figure 7.1* Guerrilla Girls, "Do Women Have to Be Naked to Get into the Met. Museum?" 1989 Photo credit, Eric Huybrechts

## Why Do We Need Feminism?

Even with so many strands of feminism, it remains a controversial term in some circles in the twenty-first century. Perhaps you are ambivalent about your own feminist identity; maybe you identify as female and grew up being told by your parents that you can do and be anything you want in this world. Perhaps you have excelled at school and athletics, surpassing brothers, male friends, and classmates in your achievements. You witness women in prominent positions in society, and you wonder why people are still talking about feminism. A brief exploration of the global statistics on gender and equality readily puts these questions at bay. Over 2.5 billion women and girls around the world are affected by discriminatory laws, often in multiple ways. In one country, for example, a woman is not recognized as a whole—but rather a half—person before the court; in another, a woman can be convicted for her own rape if she, for example, left the house without a male escort, thus putting herself at risk.[1] In 29 countries across the world, women cannot legally head their households. In 41 countries, daughters cannot inherit their parents' fortune as can sons; 32 countries have no legislation against domestic violence, and in 20 countries, perpetrators of rape can have the charges dismissed if they marry the rape survivor; around 200 million living women in 30 countries have undergone female genital mutilation; around 650 million living females were married before reaching adulthood; more than 85% of all private land is owned by men, and 40% of all countries worldwide put legal limits on women's ability to own property. Thirty percent of countries worldwide restrict women's freedom of movement.

According to the Pew Research Center, in the United States, somewhat subtler, but equally pernicious circumstances persist: about four-in-ten women in the United States (43%) say they have experienced discrimination or been treated unfairly because of their gender, including discrimination in health care, equal pay and career advancement, higher education, and public safety.[2] Not surprisingly, Native American, black, and Latina women are more likely to experience gender discrimination in these domains than white women. As these statistics exhibit, sexism is enshrined in our country's and world's institutions, laws, and norms and customs of everyday life. And yet, just as we can track the state of inequality over time and across the world, we can also track the waves of feminism.

## History of Feminisms

For most of history in the Western world, women's primary domain was the domestic one. In the nineteenth century, with the rise of the middle class, domesticity took shape prominently through the concept of the housewife. Women in this period were thus idealized as passive, nurturing, self-sacrificing, and emotional counterparts to the rationality, dominance, and coldness of men. Here as in earlier times, women functioned not only as counterparts to men, but in servitude to them, as artfully expressed by John Milton in *Paradise Lost*: "He for God only. She for God in him." The female thus adopted an altruistic role defined by purity and virtue. Her physical beauty was the outward expression of her inner goodness, which was captured in the romantic ideal of "the eternal feminine" (das Ewig Weibliche).

Nevertheless, even before the age of the housewife, a coherent feminist philosophy proliferated. Around the turn of the nineteenth century, Mary Wollstonecraft's *A Vindication of the Rights of Woman* (1792) argued for women to be granted equal opportunities in education, work, and politics. In France, Olympe de Gouges, published "Declaration of the Rights of Woman and Citizen" (*Déclaration des droits de la femme et de la citoyenne*), in which she declared woman to be man's equal and partner. Although it would be a century later that these and other prominent testimonies would inspire the first large-scale wave of feminism, they provided a meaningful foundation and a legacy to build on.

That first wave of feminism in the Western world, known as the Suffrage Movement, focused on education and political participation for women. This narrow focus, however well-intended, funneled exposure and resources to wealthy, privileged, and white women. Second wave feminism of the postwar era was similarly rooted in the discontent of college-educated mothers and housewives. Betty Friedan's famous query in

*The Feminine Mystique* lays bare the unequal circumstances of the 1950s housewife as well as the need for an intersectional feminism:

> Each suburban wife struggles with it alone. As she made the beds, shopped for groceries, matched slipcover material, ate peanut butter sandwiches with her children, chauffeured Cub Scouts and Brownies, lay beside her husband at night- she was afraid to ask even of herself the silent question—'Is this all?'[3]

Black feminists in this period, including Alice Walker, bell hooks, Mary Ann Weathers, and Michele Wallace focused on the ways in which racism and sexism are intertwined and grappled with black women's complex relationship to black men, with whom they shared a vision of civil rights and equality for people of color and whom they nevertheless sought to confront about gender inequality. Any notion of a singular feminism with unified priorities and perspectives was now in the past.

Third wave feminism, which began in the 1990s, combined characteristic elements of postmodernism in co-opting, subverting, and ironizing sexist images and stereotypes with a new skepticism about the naturalness of gender binaries. The notion that some characteristics are "male" and others "female" gave way in this period to a prevailing concept of the gender continuum, through which each of us expresses, suppresses, and—in the words of Judith Butler—performs our gender identity. Third wave feminists situated sex and sexism within a socially constructed concept of the gendered self.

For some, we are now in a fourth wave of feminist activity, catalyzed in part by the #MeToo movement, which was launched in 2006 and reached worldwide visibility after Harvey Weinstein was convicted of sexually assaulting numerous (and some prominent) women in the film and TV industry. Contemporary feminism, which has global reach, focuses on sexual harassment, body image and the media, and rape culture. Intersectional feminism is more prominent in this fourth wave, and connections between oppression based on gender, sexuality, income, race, ethnicity, and ability are more visible.

## Feminism and Music

Feminism is bound up with constructed notions of womanhood and femininity, which are embedded in all cultural production, including music. History provides no shortage of examples. In 1840, for example, Franz Schubert published a collection of interrelated songs (called a song cycle), which set to music a cycle of poems by Adelbert von Chamisso. The songs describe a woman's journey through love, marriage, and eventual loss after the death of her husband. Although Schubert probably set this cycle of poems because of its personal connection to his courtship of (and marriage to) Clara Wieck, it is notable that it does not articulate his experience, but rather hers, as the first-person narrative presents a woman's perspective through the creative voice of a man. The fourth song in the cycle, for example, "You, Ring on my Finger," describes her response to their engagement:[4]

> You, ring on my finger,
> My golden little ring,
> I press you devoutly to my lips,
> To my heart.
> I had finished dreaming
> Childhood's peaceful dream,
> I found myself alone, forlorn
> In boundless desolation.
> You, ring on my finger,
> You first taught me,
> Opened my eyes
> To life's deep eternal worth.
> I shall serve him, live for him,
> Belong to him wholly,
> Yield to him and find
> Myself transfigured in his light.
> You ring on my finger,
> My golden little ring,
> I press you devoutly to my lips,
> To my heart.

In the nineteenth century, a male-authored poem that takes a woman's perspective would have been considered progressive. Today, however, *Frauenliebe* reads as a form of puppetry by which female impersonation is used to advance sexism.

Not only do musical texts, titles, and subjects project ideas about gender, instruments themselves carry gendered meanings. In the nineteenth century in Europe, for example, the violin was widely considered to be an inappropriate instrument for female musicians because playing it could compromise a lady's presentational decorum. Gestural movements and exertions involved in playing the violin were desirable in men but not in women. Furthermore, the curvaceous, soprano-voiced violin was itself metaphorized as a "female instrument," and the bow, a sword-like symbol of power and domination, was the means of bringing "her" to sound. Nowhere is this image of the masculine conqueror of the female instrument more pronounced than in the performances of nineteenth-century Italian violinist, Niccolo Paganini. Paganini seemingly assaulted the instrument with extended techniques such as downshifting, double stops, broken octaves, legato string crossings, and left-hand pizzicato in performances that captivated massive audiences even as they disturbed them.

One hundred years later, a similar case may be made for Jimi Hendrix, whose 1968 performance of "Wild Thing" at the Monterey Pop Festival involved humping the guitar, picking it with his teeth, and then setting it on fire before smashing it to pieces. Hendrix, in this theatrical display of masculine energy, situates his guitar as the submissive—and ultimately abused—female counterpart.

Feminist musicologists, including Susan McClary and Marcia Citron, argue that many aspects of musical sound are associated with masculine ideologies of power and supremacy. Central to their arguments is the conviction that instrumental music, which has been labeled "absolute music" for its lack of referentiality, is not absolute at all, but rather instantiates and reinforces patriarchal notions of masculine dominance and feminine submission. Popular culture seems to support these associations. The protagonist Alex DeLarge in the novel/film *A Clockwork Orange* associates classical music, particularly Beethoven's ninth symphony, with rape and violence. Music and violence are so intertwined in the film that as doctors condition the protagonist against finding pleasure in brutality, he also loses

*Figure 7.2* Jimi Hendrix at the amusement park Gröna Lund in Stockholm, Sweden, May 24, 1967

his enjoyment of music. Kubrick's use of Beethoven's ninth symphony in this way must be understood as both an ironic reversal of the meaning captured by Schiller's "Ode to Joy" (which is featured in the choral finale of the symphony) and the general humanitarian *Night to Light* spirit of the work; and, at the same time, an extension of the mythology of Beethoven as a symbol of masculine energy; Beethoven, who stands "as the embodiment of musical culture itself; stern, unyielding, commanding, his name the name of the father."[5]

Of course, aggression in music is not inherently masculine. The Riot Grrl movement of the 1990s expressed the values of third wave feminism through zines, protests, and raucous, no-frills punk music, whose punishing tempos—harsh, distortion-heavy guitar riffs, and unpitched, anti-melodic vocals—carried messages about female empowerment, relationship abuse, misogyny, and a critique of the patriarchy. The energy and urgency of Riot Grrl music propelled this feminist subculture into the international spotlight.

As these examples suggest, sound is not inherently gendered; rather, gendered meanings are projected onto the music by creators and consumers. This space between the music itself and the meaning that is projected onto it is the realm of criticism.

## Feminist Criticism

Feminist criticism is, in the broadest terms, criticism that applies a feminist perspective and/or advances a feminist agenda to the description, interpretation, and evaluation of music. The first full-length book on feminist music criticism was published in 1991 by Susan McClary. The book, *Feminine Endings: Music, Gender, and Sexuality*, provided feminist analyses of over three-hundred years of music, both classical and popular. Since then, feminist criticism has ballooned into a prominent subdiscipline. Notwithstanding the diversity of feminist criticism, some general principles apply:

> **Like feminism itself, feminist criticism exhibits competing and sometimes contradictory perspectives on a given musical work or artist.**

Consider these two perspectives on Nicki Minaj's 2014 single, "Anaconda," both of which advance feminist perspectives. For Aliza Vigderman, writing for *Black Feminism*,

> Unlike some hip-hop videos in which female bodies only exist for the male gaze, Minaj creates a female-dominated world where she both controls and enjoys her sexuality. Throughout the video, Minaj is shown in erotic situations with other women, subversive in an industry with few queer women of color. In the jungle of Anaconda, Minaj explores her sexuality free from the male gaze.[6]

Prominent feminist scholar, bell hooks, however, highlights "the inability to name what we mean when we talk about feminist liberatory sexuality," labeling this a "crisis of feminist thinking."[7] For Hooks, stars like Beyoncé and Nicki Minaj may be "sexually liberating themselves against their own interests"; situating themselves within "the existing, imperialist, white supremacist, patriarchal capitalist structure of female sexuality." Of Anaconda, in specific, Hooks adopts a colloquial tone: "I was like, this s\*\*t is boring. What does it mean? Is there something that I'm missing that's happening here?"[8]

For Vigderman, Nicki Minaj transcends objectification by exhibiting agency over her own desiring body; for Hooks, by contrast, the feminist veneer of liberatory sexuality still operates from within a traditional sexist paradigm. The constructive tension between these two valid arguments characterizes the richness of contemporary feminisms.

Of course, not all feminist criticism is bound up with so much disagreement. Indeed, in highlighting women's experiences, women's contributions, women's voices, women's roles, and normative assumptions about women and womanhood, as manifest in musical works, some prominent feminist themes emerge and recur in the large body of criticism. Consider, for example, noted feminist critic Ellen Willis's 1976 review of Janis Joplin.[9] She begins by articulating the structures of power in the world that Joplin inhabited:

> [A]mong American rock performers she was second only to Bob Dylan in importance as a creator-recorder-embodiment of her generation's history and mythology. She was also the only woman to achieve that kind of stature in what was basically a male club, the only sixties culture hero to make visible and public women's experience of the quest for individual liberation, which was very different from men's.

She then goes on to highlight the normativity of the male perspective and experience, as well as the limited avenues for female expression in the male-dominated world:

> The male-dominated counterculture defined freedom for women almost exclusively in sexual terms. As a result, women endowed the idea of sexual liberation with immense symbolic importance; it became charged with all the secret energy of an as yet suppressed larger rebellion. Yet to express one's rebellion in that limited way was a painfully literal form of submission. Whether or not Janis understood that, her dual persona—lusty hedonist and suffering victim—suggested that she felt it.

Willis next highlights the cruel standards of beauty for women and stereotypes of femininity and masculinity that contextualized Joplin's self-image and experience.

> Joplin's metamorphosis from the ugly duckling of Port Arthur to the peacock of Haight-Ashbury meant, among other things, that a woman who was not conventionally pretty . . . could not only invent her own beauty . . . out of sheer energy, soul, sweetness, arrogance, and a sense of humor, but have that beauty appreciated. Not that Janis merely took advantage of changes in our notions of attractiveness; she herself changed them.

Willis goes on to explore what might have been had Joplin not died prematurely:

> Joplin's revolt against conventional femininity was brave and imaginative, but it also dovetailed with a stereotype—the ballsy, one-of-the-guys chick who is a needy, vulnerable cream puff underneath—cherished by her legions of hip male fans. It may be that she could have pushed beyond it and taken the audience with her; that was one of the possibilities that made her death an artistic as well as human disaster.

She imagines that Joplin's liberatory, female-centric sexuality may have advanced feminism by giving voice to her creations, experiences, and perspectives. Ultimately, though, she situates Joplin's music and persona within a heteronormative patriarchal context:

> Still, the songs she sang assumed heterosexual romance; it was men who made her hurt, who took another little piece of her heart . . . . Janis sang out of her pain as a woman, and men dug it. Yet it was men who caused the pain, and if they stopped causing it, they would not have her to dig. In a way their adulation was the crudest insult of all.

These themes that Willis highlights in her review—gendered power structures, the normativity of the male experience, stereotypes of femininity and womanhood, patriarchal themes, and the narrow pathways for the expression of women's experiences, perspectives, and creations—are addressed time and again in the growing body of feminist music criticism. It should also be noted that Joplin is presented here as an imperfect feminist, or perhaps, a feminist in an imperfect world. This points to another central tenet of feminist criticism, that:

> **Any musical work can be subject to feminist criticism; feminist music criticism is by no means limited to the analysis and interpretation of music that is designated feminist.**

On the contrary, a central theme of feminist criticism is to highlight normative, latent sexism in our culture. Lorraine Ali, writing for the *Los*

*Angeles Times*, labels 2019 Mötley Crüe biopic, *The Dirt*, "as vapid and sexist as the band in its heyday":

> "Girls, girls, girls." Mötley Crüe sings about them, sleeps with them, vomits on them, punches them in the face and can expect oral sex from anyone in a skirt in Netflix's astoundingly tone deaf biopic "The Dirt."
> 
> The film, which premieres Friday, is based on the group's 2001 book, "The Dirt: Confessions of the World's Most Notorious Rock Band." The book put the washed-up metal band back on the radar with lurid tales of bad-boy debauchery. In short, Mötley Crüe created a larger-than-life legacy on the backs—and bodies—of women.[10]

For Ali, the best thing about the film is that it ends, reminding the viewer that we are (were) in 2019, where "we can only hope 'The Dirt' will be buried by its own glorification of a nominally talented band's misogyny."[11]

This scathing review achieves many of the aims of the Joplin review above, highlighting the prevalence of sexism and misogyny, the silencing and stereotyping of women, the normativity of the male perspective, and the experiences of women in a patriarchal society; however, this review takes Mötley Crüe as a negative example of what's wrong with our gendered society.

Nevertheless, highlighting women's creations and experiences remains a priority of feminist criticism, and, particularly, providing women experiencing the double—or triple—oppression with positive images and models. Han Hongzheng offers a pointed review of Beyoncé's multimedia concept album, *Lemonade*, in which he draws attention to the artist's dual identity as a woman and a non-white person:

> Beyoncé's decision to include the mothers of some of the African Americans recently executed by the police (Michael Brown, Trayvon Martin, and Eric Garner) during the song *Freedom* emphasizes her commitment to address the theme of race alongside that of gender
> [. . .]
> Indeed, Beyoncé elevates mere understanding of the gender equality aspect of feminism to a more holistic level of intersectional feminism. Besides her dedication to underscore the double oppression to which black women are subjected, the pop star also engages in the creation of an optimistic model for modern femininity to which all of her viewers, regardless of race, sex, and gender, can aspire. This optimism, desperately needed in our society, fulfils the latent demand of thousands of people around the world who recognize the imbalances addressed in *Lemonade*. Besides confirming Beyoncé's excellence as a performer, the commercial success of the album demonstrates the urgency and ubiquity of the sociopolitical themes that it addresses.[12]

This last excerpt raises a final point about feminist criticism:

> Just as not all women are feminists, not all criticism by women is feminist. Similarly, not all criticism by men is excluded from the label "feminist." The gender of the critic is not a factor in determining if criticism is feminist.

According to their bio, Hongzheng uses they/them pronouns and focuses on work that engages with queer and racialized identities. Hongzheng's piece about Beyoncé would undoubtedly appeal to feminist critic, Ann Powers, who argues for critics as curators, who highlight the voices of women and other underrepresented groups:

> There's a lot of talk now about critics acting as curators, and I want to encourage all of us who interpret culture to see the politics in every curatorial act. Young women, particularly, need to hear the voices and see the faces of other women, who don't fit into the narrow roles still so common in a media world that remains patriarchal and profit driven. As some of you surely have experienced, all it takes is one Toni Morrison novel or Ani di Franco concert to set a young woman down an unexpected path.
>
> As the role of the critic and the teacher and the reporter and thinker changes, I also hope we can find new power in community. You know how feminism is supposed to be about dialogue? The conversation becomes immediate and real on message boards and in email groups, on social media sites and blogs. Use Facebook not just to show off pictures of your kids but to share reports about what's happening to women in Myanmar, or in your own hometown. Help each other.[13]

As Powers argues, we are all critics in some sense, and we can use our platforms to elevate the lives, experiences, and works of women and other marginalized groups.

## Chapter Summary

This chapter addresses two central questions: What is feminism? What constitutes feminist criticism of music? These questions are answered by analyzing canonical examples of feminist music criticism and articulating central principles of writing feminist criticism.

- Feminism encompasses competing and even contradictory agendas and concerns.
- The criteria of feminist art are contested.
- Any work of art (including music) can be subject to feminist criticism. (In other words, feminist music criticism is by no means limited to the analysis and interpretation of music that is designated feminist.)

- Feminist music criticism is concerned with women's experiences, women's contributions, women's voices, women's roles, and normative assumptions about women and womanhood, as manifest in musical works.
- Many aspects of music can reflect or symbolize ideas related to feminism and gender:
  - Instruments
  - Genres
  - Subject matter
  - Expressive elements
- Feminist criticism may highlight the following features of music:
  - Expressions of power in the public and private spheres
  - Stereotypes of femininity (and masculinity)
  - Normativity of the male perspective and experience
  - Gendered metaphors
  - Patriarchal themes
  - Women's creations, experiences, and perspectives
  - The politicization of women's experiences and women's rights

### Guide Questions

1. Why do we refer to the plural feminisms rather than the singular feminism?
2. In what sense are women's rights bound up with the rights of other minoritized groups?
3. What does Ann Powers suggest about criticism in the excerpt above? Do you agree? Justify your response.
4. Is Nicki Minaj a feminist? Does she create feminist art? Justify your responses.

### Notes

1 Caitlin Dewey, "7 Ridiculous Restrictions on Women's Rights Around the World," *Washington Post*, October 27, 2023.
2 Kim Parker and Cary Funk, "Gender Discrimination Comes in Many Forms for Today's Working Women," *Pew Research Center*, December 14, 2017, accessed July 19, 2024, https://www.pewresearch.org/short-reads/2017/12/14/gender-discrimination-comes-in-many-forms-for-todays-working-women/.
3 Betty Friedan, *The Feminine Mystique* (New York: W.W. Norton, 1963).
4 Du Ring an meinem Finger, / Mein goldenes Ringelein, / Ich drücke dich fromm an die Lippen, / Dich fromm an das Herze mein. / Ich hatt ihn ausgeträumet, / Der Kindheit friedlich schönen Traume / Ich fand allein mich, verloren / Im öden, unendlichen Raum. / Du Ring an meinem Finger / Da hast du mich erst belehrt, / Hast meinem Blick erschlossen / Des Lebens unendlichen, tiefen Wert. /

Ich will ihm dienen, ihm leben, / Ihm angehören ganz, / Hin selber mich geben und finden / Verklärt mich in seinem Glanz. / Du Ring an meinem Finger, / Mein goldenes Ringelein, / Ich drücke dich fromm an die Lippen, / Dich fromm an das Herze mein. Adelbert von Chamisso, "Du Ring an Meinem Finger," (1830), trans. by Richard Stokes, *The Book of Lieder* (London: Faber and Faber, 2005).

5 Lawrence Kramer, *After the Lovedeath: Sexual Violence and the Making of Culture* (Berkeley: University of California Press, 1997), 4–5.
6 Aliza Vigderman, "My Anaconda Don't: A Black Feminist Analysis," *Black Feminism*, April 25, 2015.
7 bell hooks, "Whose Booty Is This?" A Panel Presented at the New School, New York City, October 7, 2014, www.youtube.com/watch?v=QJZ4x04CI8c
8 Ibid.
9 Ellen Willis, "Janis Joplin," in *Beginning to See the Light: Sex, Hope, and Rock N' Roll* (Minneapolis: University of Minnesota Press, 1992), 61–67.
10 Lorraine Ali, "Review: Mötley Crüe Biopic 'The Dirt,' as Vapid and Sexist as the Band in Its Heyday," *Los Angeles Times*, March 21, 2019, accessed July 2, 2023, https://www.chicagotribune.com/2019/03/21/the-dirt-review-mtley-cre-biopic-as-vapid-and-sexist-as-the-band-in-its-heyday/.
11 Ibid.
12 Han Hongzheng, "Smashing Windows: Beyoncé's Lemonade, Intersectional Feminism, and Black Empowerment," *IFA Contemporary*, April 19, 2018, accessed August 9, 2023, https://ifacontemporary.org/smashing-windows-beyonces-lemonade-intersectional-feminism-and-black-empowerment/.
13 Ann Powers, "YOU BETTER THINK: Why Feminist Criticism Still Matters in a Post-Feminist, Peer to Peer World," *Tenth Annual USC Women in Higher Education Luncheon*, University of Southern California, March 10, 2009.

# 8 Queer Music Criticism

The LGBTQ+ community denotes the shared experiences, priorities, and concerns of people who identify as lesbian, gay, bisexual, transgender, and/or queer. Queer advocates argue against the notion that heterosexual desire is normal or correct; that gender and sexuality are correlated and fixed; and that biology and identity are interdependent. Rather, queer advocates focus on social, political, and cultural forces that structure and reinforce gender and sexual normativity. They work to bring awareness and visibility to queer people, their lived experience, and their continued disenfranchisement in society.

A central locus of queer activism is Pride; across the globe, LGBTQ+ advocates come together annually to affirm each other's identities and experiences at celebratory parades and other community events. Pride, however, encompasses more than annual celebrations; Pride symbolizes the affirmation of queer identity in the face of persistent religious, legal, social, and political persecution. Before 1969, the life of an LGBTQ+ person in the United States was lived under the shroud of secrecy, as any public expression of queer identity (such as holding hands with someone of the same sex) was illegal. Gay clubs and bars provided refuge and community for LGBTQ+ people who experienced alienation under these prejudicial laws. The 1969 Stonewall Riots, which grew in response to a police raid of a gay bar in Greenwich Village called the Stonewall Inn, catalyzed queer communities in the United States and abroad, and activism came to adopt a more public form. Groups such as the Human Rights Campaign, the National Gay and Lesbian Task Force, and the ACT UP AIDS Coalition (all active today) brought visibility to queer communities and fought for legal and political reform over the decades that followed. The pride flag emerged as an iconic symbol of the struggles and victories of the LGBTQ+ community. (Before the flag, a pink triangle symbolized pride in some communities; it was adapted from a badge that gay prisoners were forced to wear in Nazi concentration camps.) The iconic rainbow flag has been expanded in recent decades to articulate the diversity of identities within the queer community.

DOI: 10.4324/9780429505171-12

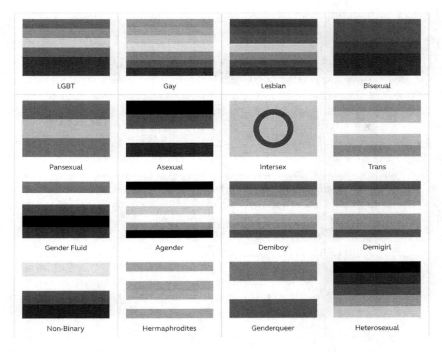

*Figure 8.1* Pride flags
Source: Photo credit, *Валя Беляев*

## Genderqueer

Gender non-conformity is an increasing locus of queer advocacy in the twenty-first century. Concepts like manly, feminine, girly, maternal, and macho conjure shared images in our culture. Although the nature versus nurture debate remains unresolved in the public consciousness, the scientific community provides clear evidence that we nurture normative behaviors and attitudes about masculinity and femininity: in double blind studies, parents' descriptions of their one-day-old infants consistently fell along traditional gender binaries; children's clothing, toys, and behavioral reinforcements all conditioned young children toward traditional constructs of gender.[1] These constructs are pernicious not only because they define normalcy, legitimacy, and dominant culture; they also reinforce a system of patriarchy, in which cisgendered, heterosexual males are granted unearned political, material, and social advantage over other identity groups.

South African musician, actor, and writer, Nakhane, is one genderqueer artist who uses their talent to connect the personal to the political. This review by Tope Olufemi connects Nakhane's personal identity to the "tangles" of history in a revealing discussion of the artist's music:

> It's the week before the Christmas lull when Nakhane joins me for our Zoom conversation, just a few days before the release of their latest EP, *Leading Lines*. I've spent the preceding morning with the EP, talking in all that the South African musician, actor and novelist has to say. Our conversation extends all of those musical conversations far beyond a song's three-minute mark. After all, queer always has something to say.
>
> "The music that everyone's hearing now has been ready for so long," they tell me, noting that much of it came before they identified as non-binary. They speak slowly, with care and enthusiasm. "So, now, when I listen to the songs, some of the, 'gendered characters' in the music, I wish they were less binary. But it is a product of the time when I was writing it. That's queerness I suppose, it influences everything and nothing."
>
> Everything and nothing is a concise description of "queer" as a process, or a state of being. Any understanding of queerness within popular music will touch on both absence (blacklisting, violence, erasure) and presence, both in the literal form of queer icons and the undercurrent of queer that passes through the music and fashion of the 80s and 90s, for example. Nakhane's awareness of those that came before them runs through their music, taking heavy inspiration from the slick, glittery guitars and synths of the 80s and combining this with heavier, club-ready sounds.
>
> "For me, queerness is seeing a new perspective, seeing things from a different way. And not necessarily answering things but experimenting", they tell me as their eyes light up. Queer has always upturned, unseated and is "always forging forward, or left!", they say—tying together the existence of their work with queer theory at large. Their analysis quietly reminds me that they see themselves as part of something larger.
>
> By that definition, Nakhane's work is delightfully "queer", easily imbuing the upbeat grooves of South African house and dance music with emotional weight, before swinging that weight over their head with flurries of wit and charisma. "Tell Me Your Politik", a song about regretting having sex with someone with differing political views, exorcises personal demons while showcasing Nakhane's intriguing balance between dark and light—backing the line "everyone is a murderer" with big, wide basses, synth swells and handclaps. It's music that doesn't mind chewing up convention before spitting out something entirely different.
>
> [. . .]
>
> Politics does not bleed into their music as much as it is its basis; the two are not disentangled. Their music has been laden with political themes, which often revolve around Nakhane's own personal

experiences of homophobia and queerphobia during their upbringing in South Africa, after they were outed. Despite the repression they felt, they remain aware of the freeing aspects of queerness.

"If anything, we're saying that everyone should be able to do whatever the fuck they want, as long as they're not hurting people." The rejection of this freedom is a point of curiosity. "Why is that freedom so scary? That's that freedom I'm after, artistically, personally, romantically . . . I'm interested in that hunger for experiencing, hunger for openness, hunger for finding something else!" Their eyes are alight again. "So many people I love lives have been thwarted because they felt like they couldn't do anything, because the consequences are so dire."

As much as queer drives forward, it also finds itself tangled up in its own history—just like Nakhane themselves. I ask them how they've been since they moved to London five years ago. History can also be baggage, and its duality as a place of comfort and pain becomes clear. "Every piece of work that I make, every song that I write carries with it inchoate . . . relationships, things I haven't dealt with properly. Things I haven't closed, things that still need closure!—I guess maybe that's why I write about it," they say. "So it's very multifaceted, and then on the other hand, it's very simple—it's just a song."[2]

## Queering the Patriarchy

The oppression of sexual- and genderqueer people has been connected to the legitimization of the patriarchy. Numerous studies have confirmed the relationship between a belief in and support of traditional gender roles and anti-queer prejudice. In Karin Martin's research, for example, "the intertwining of gender and sexuality" was revealed as "an attempt to create a mechanism for controlling and keeping in check the gender hierarchy, which was dependent on a particular set of sexual relations."[3] In this sense, Feminism and LGBTQ+ advocates share perspectives, concerns, and values. Indeed, you'll recall that a central tenant of third wave feminism was increasing skepticism about the category of womanhood. Before the twentieth century, the term *gender* was typically used to refer to words in language cultures that have feminine, masculine, and neutral articles (For example, *la voiture* is French for car, and the German *das Brot* means bread.) The psychologist Robert Stoller is credited with adopting the term "gender" to refer to behavioral traits and experiences across the spectrum of femininity and masculinity and "sex" to refer to biological characteristics of a person. By uncoupling gender and sex, Stoller was able to articulate the experience of transgender people and, in the process, denaturalize normative ideas about women and womanhood. In this sense, he continued the work of feminists like Simone de Beauvoir, who began her seminal *The Second Sex* (1949) by stating that "one is not born but rather becomes a woman." Though written over seven decades ago, these words articulate a central priority of queer theory and advocacy as well as a nexus point between feminism and the LGBTQ+ community.

**Music and Queer Expression**

Music has long been a site of queer expression; since the 1960s, genres such as disco, EDM, and Broadway have been associated with queer artists and queer culture. Even rock music of the 1960s and '70s, typically associated with sexism and machismo, featured androgyny, most notably in a subgenre called glam rock, whose performers wore elaborate costumes, make up, and glitter in a visual style that undermined gender normativity. Historians and scholars have credited glam rockers with achieving a freeing of rigid gender stereotypes, a loosening of the "sexed male subject from previous, more predictable moorings,"[4] the "embrace of the prototypically feminine,"[5] the creation of "new possibilities,"[6] and the provision of a "space for alternative sexual definitions and an openness to sexuality to include both the heterosexual and homosexual."[7] The subversive visual and performance style of these artists harnessed the power of camp.

"Ostentatious, exaggerated, affected, theatrical; effeminate or homosexual; pertaining to, characteristic of, homosexuals." These words, from 1902, comprise the first definition of "camp" in the *Oxford English Dictionary*. Historians often point to Oscar Wilde as the full expression of the aesthetic: "It was Wilde's stigmatized body, whose trials for 'gross indecency' in 1895 typified the 'homosexual', which provided a grammar of camp as a twisted form of aestheticism that largely (if indirectly) meant sexual deviance."[8] Camp has been identified by queer theorists as a key strategy of resistance against heteronormative ideology. The exaggeration, theatricality, incongruity, humor, and absurdity that camp aesthetics promotes serve to undermine the legitimacy straight culture.

The camp-style of glam rockers of the sixties and seventies aligned with the Gay Liberation Movement, the increasing openness about sexuality in the mass media, and ultimately, the unhinging of the normative gender stereotypes of the previous generation, to challenge the norms of male sexuality and pave the way for a more progressive, inclusive, heterogeneous sexual and gender paradigm. David Bowie's glam aesthetic is thus described in terms of "images of resistance," and attributed to the creation of new possibilities and more "imaginative and expressive potentials" than those that were available in society at large.[9]

Although glam rock would not completely overturn the well-entrenched sexual ideology of society, it nevertheless "widened the reach of the public imagination and [became] a permanent interlocutor in pop's future."[10]

*Figure 8.2* David Bowie performing at the Tower Theater in Upper Darby, PA, during the Diamond Dogs Tour, July 1974

**Camp Isn't Always Queer**

However, androgyny and camp are not always subversive, feminist, or queer. Consider, for example, The Rolling Stones. The fact of Mick Jagger's incorporation of feminine stereotypes into his aesthetic needs little comment: around the turn of the 1970s, Jagger could be found in a nurse's outfit, a ballerina costume, pearls, and/or makeup, seemingly confounding the machismo style of rock 'n' roll for which The Rolling Stones were known. He presents arguably the first full-scale androgynous persona to reach a mass youth audience through rock 'n' roll; as such, discussions of the lineage of androgyny in rock music invariable note Mick Jagger as an important link in the chain. Mick Jagger's music and performance style exist on two levels, the first being characterized by *machismo*. This term, which is defined as "a strong or exaggerated sense of manliness; an assumptive attitude that virility, courage, strength, and entitlement to dominate are attributes or concomitants of masculinity," profoundly understates and ignores the pernicious, misogynistic content of The Rolling Stones music and imagery: the Hollywood billboard for *Black and Blue*, in which a bound and gagged woman proclaims, "I'm black and blue from the Rolling Stones and I love it," provides a better example of the gender and sexual presentation of the band.

The secondary level of communication is related to the visual image of androgyny that is gradually incorporated into The Rolling Stones' aesthetic. However, even the proponents of The Rolling Stones' camp aesthetic acknowledge that it is couched in "the suggestion of masquerade and play,"[11] and that it functions mainly to "ridicule female stereotypes" and thereby "underscore their [the band's] basic machismo."[12] By parodying females through androgyny, The Rolling Stones worked to cement, rather than undermine, gender normativity and patriarchal sexism. In this sense, Mick Jagger's androgyny isn't queer because it doesn't, in the end, destabilize normative categories of gender and sexuality.

Not all performative queer expression is as sinister as Mick Jagger's has been deemed to be; however, queer expression without queer identity or allyship can be cause for skepticism. Even allyship can sometimes be met with skepticism. Consider, for example, Taylor Swift's queer anthem, "You Need to Calm Down." The video features prominent queer celebrities, including Ellen DeGeneres, RuPaul, and Laverne Cox, and a bubble gum camp aesthetic that clarifies *who* needs to calm down, as well as *why*.

In a unique, multi-vocal review in *The New York Times*, three critics articulate why Swift's song has been met with mixed reviews. For pop music critic, Jon Carimanica,

> The rollout of Swift's seventh album, "Lover," which is due in August, has been awash in rainbow-themed imagery, and Swift is speaking directly on a matter of political and social import—LGBTQ rights. It's a topic she had barely acknowledged before last October, when she formally endorsed two Democratic candidates, declaring on Instagram, "I cannot vote for someone who will not be willing to fight for dignity for ALL Americans, no matter their skin color, gender or who they love."
>
> But when it comes to making public statements in support of these issues, Taylor waited a relatively long time: until after Katy Perry, after Lady Gaga, after Kacey Musgraves. Presumptions of her progressivism notwithstanding, in a time when speaking out has become a critical component of celebrity, the silence was extremely loud.

And so when you are, relatively speaking, late to the game, you have to bet big. Having a video as chock-full of gay celebrities and drag queens as this (as well as the one beyond-critique gesture of 2019: a cameo from Billy Porter) is a worthy celebration, but it is also plausible cover.

Acknowledging that it is indeed "big," *New York Times* critic Wesley Morris argues that it is self-serving and shallow:

> But Jon, it's all gesture. I love Billy Porter as much as the planet does at the moment. But what are his three seconds meant to do? What are *any* of the L.G.B.T.Q.I.A.-identified people in this video—DeGeneres, Adam Lambert, the "Queer Eye" guys, to start—meant to signify? This is as much a music video as it is a detonated rainbow-flag piñata . . . the riot of auxiliary personalities [sic]—*gay* personalities—are in the service of her brand and persona. No one else's stardom or skill has more to do than endorse hers.

Ultimately, for Morris,

> It's Pride month, and all of that flamboyant Willy Wonkaness is meant to signal to the viewer—louder and more *shablamingly* than the song itself—that Swift supports and loves each letter in the queer alphabet. (Do you guys think she should have saved the spelling in the first single, "Me!," for this song?) I think I'd rather have this than the tolerance lecture of, say, Macklemore & Ryan Lewis and Mary Lambert's "Same Love."
>
> But there's also something either tired, tardy or tidily opportunistic about this video. It's shown up at a moment when corporations are spending June bleeding the colors of the rainbow flag, when store windows announce that all orientations are welcome, when the avatar for your pending Uber has turned gay. I don't doubt the core sincerity or commercial power of any of this. Maybe it makes it more impossible for the bakeries of the world to deny queer customers a wedding cake.

Carmonica agrees:

> If she's been a supporter of progressive social causes, she's had a phenomenally huge platform for a decade now, but has barely leveraged it. You mentioned Madonna, and Caryn, you spoke about Gaga—in both cases, their embrace of marginalized and oppressed groups was central to their aesthetic position from the earliest days of their careers. They

134   *Critical Lenses*

portrayed the kinship as natural, which is why, by comparison, what's on display here feels strenuous.

For Ganz, similarly,

there are different shades of allyship and enduring questions about who "gets" to be an ally, or a gay icon, and how—are allies only chosen by the gay community or can they be imposed from beyond, and is there a way for both to do important work? Conveniently, two opposing examples arrived at the same moment on Monday: Swift's "You Need to Calm Down" video and Robyn's "Ever Again" clip, inverses in nearly every way.

Taylor's video is a kandy-kolored fantasyscape populated by 29 other personalities. Robyn's has a palate of blues, greens and browns; her only co-star is a microphone stand. Taylor's is a series of meticulously interlaced scenes and narratives; Robyn's features nothing but the singer dancing and dragging herself through the sand. Swift's video screams about gay rights (and female pop star rights). Robyn's doesn't say a word. But that doesn't make it less gay; Robyn has always showed, not told. Beloved gay pop isn't always wrapped in rainbows, but in exuberance, rawness, poise, virtuosity—the audacity of radiating absolute emotional freedom.[13]

To be sure, camp still has its place in queer aesthetics; however, as this reviewer states, camp is not the only way of articulating LGBTQ+ identity and pride in the twenty-first century.

## Queer Isn't Always Camp

Today, LGBTQ+ artists sing country music, hip-hop, pop, punk, and every other popular genre with increasing openness, authenticity, and sincerity. Frank Ocean provides an important example of the mainstreaming of queer identity and the sincerity movement in queer expression. Consider, for example, this review of Frank Ocean and Queer R&B, which highlights Ocean's search for authenticity amidst the "hypersaturation" of the "music industry machine":[14]

"A jack-in-the-box, a Fabergé gem, a clockwork toy, a chess problem, an infernal machine, a trap to catch viewers, a cat-and-mouse game . . ." This isn't the tagline of Frank Ocean's new album *Blond(e)*, but Mary McCarthy's far-sighted 1962 review of Nabokov, which effortlessly describes another innovative masterpiece that similarly refuses to be pigeonholed. Just as the genre-bending *Pale Fire* isn't simply a "novel", Ocean's latest output hardly deserves to be called an "album" alone—more like a fully-fledged pop culture event, following other much-hyped recent releases from Beyoncé, Kanye West and Rihanna, to name a few.

But unlike them, Frank Ocean—the man and the myth—invites a whole new level of scrutiny. Ever since the widely circulated 2012 open letter that revealed his painful, unrequited love for another man, the most reluctant mainstream pop star of our time has shrouded his activities in almost total obscurity. Traces occasionally surfaced here and there: a smattering of guest vocal appearances (such as on *The Life of Pablo*), whispers of secret listening parties hosted in New York, a Calvin Klein ad that looks like it could have been lifted straight from his cryptic Tumblr blog.

All the while, diehard fans congregating on Twitter and Reddit descended on any morsels of speculation they could find, including hints from his former producer Malay and since-deleted Instagram posts from collaborators Lil B and Nabil. By following these vanishing internet paper trails, they were only recreating what everyone had tried to do with the notable male pronouns in the lyrics of his previous release, *channel ORANGE*—only this time, in Ocean's real life.

After exploring Ocean's image, the reviewer turns to his music, which is seen to "swerve along the queer, digressive path, forever eluding his audience in ways that are as fascinating as they are maddening":

Nonetheless, in both life and art, Frank is everywhere and nowhere, an absent presence who commands yet shuns the media hyper-saturation that the music industry machine demands of its stars. He's the artist who writes himself and his queerness in and out of his work, enticing the listener down seductive musical rabbit-holes only to deny them any concrete explanations. The confessional queer speaker from *channel ORANGE* who plaintively cries "I could never make him love me" on "Bad Religion" seems unusually absent on *Blond(e)*. Apart from "Good Guy" which tersely sketches out a failed date at a "gay bar", there are no explicit references to a specifically male lover elsewhere in the album, although it has plenty of passing nods to sex and erotic desire.

To detangle these shadowy half-clues on Frank Ocean's sexuality, then, we would need to look further afield. In this respect, Ocean may have provided us with the biggest clue of all via his decision to drop an unexpected visual album without any context, *Endless*, as well as a magazine, *Boys Don't Cry* alongside *Blond(e)*. Working across a variety of media, Ocean lets his strong aesthetic sensibility reveal yet another layer of coded signs for us to analyse endlessly, if you'll excuse the pun. Added to the ambiguous duality of the album's title *Blond*—or *Blonde*, as it's shown on Apple Music—Ocean is practically demanding that we mustn't fall into the trap of taking his music entirely at face value, of pinning a neat, singular resolution on the enigmatic collage of impressions and fragments that's been presented to us. Instead of spoonfeeding us an explicit, straightforward answer, his art prefers to swerve along the queer, digressive path, forever eluding his audience in ways that are as fascinating as they are maddening.

Intriguingly, even as Ocean's music is confessional, intimate, and authentic, it's coded in such a way as to invite listeners to interpret its meaning "however we wish:"

> This tantalising possibility of ambiguous, interchangeable male and female love objects invites us to imagine these shadowy half-lovers however we wish—even if they turn out to be a hopeless fantasy of the lovelorn speaker. "What could I do to know you better than I do now?" repeats the outro to "Alabama", while he promises that "I'll be the boyfriend in your wet dreams tonight" on album highlight "Self Control". For every desperate plea of love that's proffered, there is a hasty retraction, an offhand shrug: "Been living in an idea/An idea from another man's mind", he reveals on "Seigfried". "Ivy" contains another revelation disguised in the banal: "I broke your heart last week/You'll probably feel better by the weekend". Even a line that leaves nothing to the imagination, such as "All this drillin' got the dick feelin' like a power tool" from "Comme Des Garçons", buries a double entendre that could refer to him or a male lover (the "power tool").
>
> A master of endless contradictions, Frank Ocean wrong-foots the listener time and time again, forcing them to re-examine their presumptions of what love songs should (or shouldn't) be. His art not only bleeds from one genre and medium to another, but is also fluid in its portrayals of gender and sexuality. "Dynamic" is the only word he used to describe his sexuality in a 2012 *GQ* interview, and this prescient attitude to self-definition is almost fully accepted as gospel by the Tumblr generation in 2016.
>
> His distaste for neat, fixed identity categories—"You can't feel a box. You can't feel a label."—seems to have paved the way for many queer and gender non-conforming young black creatives in the public eye right now: think Angel Haze, Young Thug, Jaden Smith and Amandla Stenberg, for instance. Beyond these inspiring figures, even straight-identifying male R&B artists such as Kanye West, Blood Orange

and Chance the Rapper are daring to show new forms of masculinity in their avant-garde, emotionally indulgent recent works.

So while Frank Ocean is certainly not making some kind of torch-bearing LGBT liberation statement in his latest releases, they are no less powerful and visionary for aligning his queerness—even if it is highly coded and enigmatic—with the experimental, boundary-pushing mood that's taken hold of so much mainstream R&B right now. This subtly hinted version of queerness is almost like a modern variation on the flamboyant displays of queer sexuality from other androgynous male icons of music history, including Prince (who Frank eulogised in a moving Tumblr statement) and David Bowie (who features prominently in *Boys Don't Cry*).

Ocean's music doesn't exist purely in a queer echo-chamber, though. He combines these influences with numerous cherrypicked name-drops and quotes from an eclectic variety of "straight" sources such as The Beatles, The Fugees, Trayvon Martin and even Elliot Smith. But the way he deftly interweaves queer and straight, male and female, mainstream and counterculture, leaving these binaries much less clear than how he found them, is an essentially queer act in itself. His work follows in the footsteps of other visionary queer masterpieces such as Walt Whitman's *Leaves of Grass*, which also asks to "discover me so by faint indirections,/ And when I meet you mean to discover you by the like in you".

Looking ahead to the future, the queerness of *Blond(e)* is almost certain to inspire a new generation of boundary-breaking artists (and more importantly, queer people of colour) who want to emerge from the long shadow cast by centuries of widespread homophobia, fear and ignorance over LGBT issues. It's encouraging to see that defining yourself the way you wish to be defined and coming out on your own terms is becoming the new normal—both in the music world and in real life. Hopefully one day, gender fluidity will become as commonly accepted as genre fluidity, and straight artists such as Lady Gaga and Macklemore will not dominate the face of the LGBT liberation cause via their so-called queer anthems.

Above all, the personal expressions of queerness found in Frank Ocean's art are remarkable in how intangible, fluid and elusive they remain, much to the dismay of homophobes. This messy contradictoriness in art and in life—a façade that's ironically well constructed—is an essential part of his appeal, and is what makes his music so fresh and endlessly compelling to listeners both straight and queer, out and closeted. The only conclusion that we can now attempt to draw perhaps comes from Frank's words alone. Musing on his fascination with cars in *Boys Don't Cry*, the reluctant spokesperson reveals a mission statement of sorts: "Maybe it links to a deep subconscious straight boy fantasy. Consciously though, I don't want straight—a little bent is good."

This critic celebrates the queerness of *Blond*, which unsettles the received binaries of straight and queer, male and female, out and closeted.

### Queer Criticism as History and Allyship

As we've seen, queer criticism may be described as criticism that engages with queer-coded strategies of resistance to heteronormative structures and systems in society. Queer criticism is a form of advocacy, in that it brings attention to the experiences and expressions of queer people in a knowledgeable, informed, and helpful way. Consider this review of Zebra Katz, "Ima Read" by Hermione Hoby, in which the critic explores the subversive (and political) meanings behind "Ima Read":

> this isn't just about literacy ("I'm gonna take that bitch to college/I'm gonna give that bitch some knowledge") but a homage to the ballroom scene of New York—the world of voguing and drag culture immortalised in Jennie Livingston's 1990 documentary, *Paris is Burning*. "Read", in that context, means to cut someone down to size, to flex your bitchiness.[15]

Still, as other interviewers and critics have noted, Morgan prefers his characters to remain opaque:

> "People are still finding out who Zebra Katz is," he says. "Each song will shed a little more light. Is he sinister? Is he a villain?" My ears perk up at the villain part. I ask if he thinks Zebra Katz has any responsibility within this particular movement. He's thoughtful. "I am going from project to project. I don't really even think about that. I am glad it's happening and that people are talking about it, and the music I make may be influenced by those thoughts and opinions but I am making art that is my own, and for the joy of making it."[16]

For Ian Grittis at the *Guardian*, opacity and vapidity are two sides of the same coin:

> Musically, his sludgy, house-inflected beats are mostly minimal, a platform for his preening and posturing, but occasionally hit on a sharp tune. [. . .]
> For now, Zebra Katz is a deeply entertaining, painfully hip art-house novelty act. Whether he becomes any more than that is another question entirely.[17]

Nonetheless, there seems to be a mission and message behind everything Morgan produces. This discussion of his dissertation project reveals the subtle (and subtly political) message that lies beneath the surface:

> In a nutshell, my senior thesis was called "Moor Contradictions" and as someone who has been studying theater for a majority of their life, I was always trying to tackle the idea of colorblind casting. There are very few black references in Shakespeare outside of Othello being a Moor. I looked at the Moors in Shakespeare and these monolithic black characters like the "thug" or the "police officer" or the "angry black man." Having gone to study Shakespeare at the British-American Drama Academy, I had to tackle that and try to get my professors to see that. We could re-interpret these words in such a way that actually does something and means something. So, I took that and I went back to Eugene Lang and instead of doing *Three Sisters* or *Uncle Vanya* by Chekhov, I wanted to do my own work. I created "Moor Contradictions" and Zebra Katz was one of several characters within that piece.[18]

In drawing out these subtly political messages in Katz's music, critics position their work as political in its own right, supporting and elevating the voices of minoritized artists.

## Chapter Summary

This chapter addresses two central questions: What is queer theory? What constitutes queer music criticism? The chapter analyzes canonical examples of queer music criticism and then establishes central principles of queer criticism. The main points of the chapter are as follows:

- Queer theory uncouples and interrogates normative relationships between sex, gender, and desire.
- Historically, the abstractness and non-specificity of musical language has rendered it a rich and problematic space for encoding queer experience.
- Musical forms, instruments, styles, scales and modes, and other elements of music can project normative or queer ideologies.
- The aesthetics of camp have been wielded as an aesthetics of resistance.
- Queer criticism is particularly concerned with the breakdown of binary relationships, which can metaphorize normative sexual and gender identities.

## Guide Questions

1. How does the word "pride" capture the experiences of gender and sexual non-conforming people in the 20th and 21st centuries?
2. How might "camp" manifest in musical sound? Justify your answer.

140  *Critical Lenses*

3. Why do you think particular musical genres have been historically associated with queer expression?
4. Should queer criticism be created exclusively by queer people? Justify your answer.

**Notes**

1. Josh L. Boe and Rebecca J. Woods, "Parents' Influence on Infants' Gender-Typed Toy Preferences," *Sex Roles* 79, no. 5–6 (2018): 358–373.
2. Tope Olufemi, "Not Done: An Interview with Nakhane," *The Quietus*, January 9, 2023, accessed July 19, 2024, https://thequietus.com/interviews/nakhane-interview/.
3. Karin A. Martin, "Becoming a Gendered Body: Practices of Preschools," *American Sociological Review* 63, no. 4 (August 1998): 494–511.
4. Ian Chambers, *Urban Rhythms: Pop Music and Popular Culture* (New York: St. Martin's Press, 1985), 113.
5. Mike Kelley, "Cross Gender/Cross Genre," *PAJ* 22, no. 1 (January 2000): 64.
6. Chambers, Ibid., 135–136.
7. Sheila Whiteley, "Little Red Rooster vs. the Honky Tonk Woman: Mick Jagger, Sexuality, Style, and Image," in *Sexing the Groove: Popular Music and Gender* (London: Routledge, 1997), 75.
8. Joobin Bekhrad, "What Does It Mean to be Camp?" *BBC Culture*, May 7, 2019, accessed June 23, 2024, https://www.bbc.com/culture/article/20190503-what-does-it-mean-to-be-camp.
9. Ian Chambers, *Urban Rhythms: Pop Music and Popular Culture* (New York: St. Martin's Press, 1985), 136.
10. Ibid.
11. Whitely, Ibid., 77.
12. Barney Hoskyns, *Glam! Bowie, Bolan and the Glitter Rock Revolution* (New York: Pocket Books, 1998), 12.
13. Jon Caramanica, Wesley Morris, and Caryn Ganz, "For Taylor Swift, Is Ego Stronger Than Pride?: Three Writers Discuss Her 'You Need to Calm Down' Video, Which Is Populated with L.G.B.T.Q. Celebrities. Not Everyone Sees It as a Celebration," *New York Times*, June 18, 2019, accessed May 14, 2024, https://www.nytimes.com/2019/06/18/arts/music/taylor-swift-you-need-to-calm-down-video.html.
14. Laurie Chen, "The Artist Is Absent: Frank Ocean's Coded Queerness," *The Quietus*, August 30, 2016, accessed May 2, 2024, https://thequietus.com/opinion-and-essays/black-sky-thinking/frank-ocean-queer-blond/.
15. Hermione Hoby, "Zebra Katz: Creating a Strong, Black, Queer Male Is Something That Needed to Happen," *The Guardian*, May 25, 2013, accessed September 12, 2023, www.theguardian.com/music/2013/may/25/zebra-katz-interview-ima-read.
16. Deb Doing Dallas, "Dallas Observer Zebra Katz: 'Ballroom Culture Has Been Available for Years, But It's Still Very Much a Subculture," *Dallas Observer*, July 25, 2012, accessed June 21, 2023, https://www.dallasobserver.com/music/zebra-katz-ballroom-culture-has-been-available-for-years-but-its-still-very-much-a-subculture-7059098.
17. Ian Gittins, "Zebra Katz—Review," *The Guardian*, June 9, 2013, accessed May 12, 2023, https://www.theguardian.com/music/2013/jun/09/zebra-katz-review.
18. Matt Moen, "Zebra Katz Talks Berghain, Brooklyn, and Shakespeare," *Paper Magazine*, April 7, 2020, accessed June 22, 2023, https://www.papermag.com/interview-zebra-katz-less-is-moor.

# 9 Postcolonialism and Critical Race Theory

1782 marked the premiere of Mozart's musical drama, *The Abduction from the Seraglio*, (*Die Entfuhrung aus dem Serail*), which was commissioned by the Austrian emperor, Joseph II to commemorate the 100-year anniversary of the failed Turkish siege on Vienna. The three-act *Singspiel* (a German opera-like genre that incorporates spoken word) recounts a classic love and rescue tale whose urgency is premised on the predatory lust of the captors, Turkish pirates, whom Mozart caricatures through crude and transparent musical devices.

Osmin—servant to the Turkish noble, Selim Pasha—is rendered comic from his very first notes, which he sings from the depths of a cavernous bass voice. Though the piece begins sweetly, it builds tension in step with Osmin's increasing annoyance at his captive's mild interjections. A jarring metric and tempo modulation square in the middle of the final couplet ultimately reveals sweetness as a foil for Osmin's flaring and uncontrolled temper. When, at the close of his piece, Osmin finally acknowledges the source of his annoyance, he displays his stupidity with repeated inquiries of "eh," after which he unveils a confused litany of tortures that *begins* with death. In this—already his second—aria, blunt, clipped phrases, whose cold, grammatical treatment (through static repetition or rigid sequential motion) lacks invention and refinery, pointedly depict his brutish persona. His rage, as Mozart boasted in a letter to his father, is "rendered comic through the use of Turkish music"—including rigidly triadic motion interspersed with jutting chromatic distortions and jarring *forte* incursions with crashing bass drums and cymbals. While these sounds invoke the traditional Turkish military music that explicitly frames the opera, other moments convey a more generic sense of alterity.

Consider the opening of this aria: the static, almost ritualistic repetition of a single note finds it only relief in a menacing chromatic inflection that completes the phrase and, with it, the conflation of monotony and dissonance that so aptly depicts Osmin's primitive alterity. Here as elsewhere, Osmin's character (and, through him, otherness itself) is associated with the blunt

DOI: 10.4324/9780429505171-13

major triad and march-like tempo and meter (borrowed from Janissary military music), neighbor-note dissonances, abrupt forte/piano alternation, distant and unprepared modulations, and a cavernous bass voice, which is explicitly featured in a chromatically inflected descending motive, first set to the words "until you swear to obey me" (bis du zu gehorchen mir schwörst).

The captives, Belmonte and Constanze, represent the Western norm against which Osmin's alterity is defined. They receive the only traditional operatic arias, and their Enlightened reason is transmitted through mellifluous songs. When the opera is historically located at the hundred-year anniversary of the failed (though threatening) Turkish siege of Vienna; at, moreover, a time of renewed tension among Turkey and Austria, the curious intermingling of drama and buffoonery emerge as a blatant "appeal to the emperor" through which Mozart "declare[d] his support for the dynamic promise of Enlightened absolutism":[1] the Turkish characters served Joseph II's containment strategies toward the Ottoman Empire, while the reason and civility of the Western counterparts reinforced the tenets of reason and civility that operated at home.

### Orientalism

Mozart's *The Abduction from the Seraglio*, which is still performed today, offers a striking example of what historian and scholar, Edward Said, labeled *Orientalism*. In his groundbreaking work, Said characterized Orientalism as a Western fantasy about the so-called Orient that serves colonial interests in Europe and North America. The use of the term "Orient" deliberately captures the erasure of important cultural distinctions across Central, South, and East Asia; North Africa; and the Middle East. Unique religions, languages, geographies, political structures, and histories are reduced to bald stereotypes that reflect the colonial and imperialist tendencies in Europe (and, later, the United States) from the eighteenth century onward. In the realm of studio art, 1827 *The Death of Sardanapalus* (*La Mort de Sardanapale*) by Eugéne Delacroix is often cited as exemplifying this mindset: the painting depicts the ancient Assyrian king lounging with a nonplussed affect amidst a cornucopia of violence, gluttony, immodesty, and material excess.

As these examples illustrate, Orientalism is a type of othering. To be sure, all human societies formulate ideas of the other; it serves a natural, subconscious process of defining and legitimating our own identities. In the history of the Western world, however, that othering is complicated by colonialism, which is defined as the establishment, exploitation, acquisition, and expansion of one territory, people, or country by another. The desire to exploit and conquer has fused with propagandistic notions of the other, which is thus characterized as weak, sadistic, savage, immoral,

*Figure 9.1* Costume Study for Osmin in the Abduction from the Seraglio by W.A. Mozart, drawing, Johann Georg Christoph Fries

feminine, and/or primitive. Even twentieth-century artists who valorized so-called primitive societies, such as Gaugin, whose Tahitian paintings celebrate the "great rustic-superstitious simplicity" of his subjects,[2] nevertheless prefer them as undifferentiated and romanticized fantasies that put

*Figure 9.2* La Mort de Sardanapole, Eugéne Delacroix, 1827

industrial, modern selfhood into relief. Indeed, whether overtly negative or not, the category of the non-Western "other" reliably misrepresents its subject because it takes as its vantage point the righteous Western self.

### Postcolonialism

Said's central claim, that Western discourse about the so-called Orient since the eighteenth century has been "a systematic discourse by which Europe was able to manage—even produce—the Orient politically, sociologically, militarily, ideologically, scientifically, and imaginatively,"[3] catalyzed the intellectual movement known as postcolonialism. Postcolonial theory refers to the critical engagement with the legacy of colonialism and imperialism worldwide and the impact of human control and exploitation (including slavery). It seeks to make visible and interrogate global power structures that are proliferated and propagandized through politics, culture, and the media.

Popular culture, seemingly removed from political theory, provides evidence of both contemporary colonialism and postcolonial critique. For example, Katy Perry's 2013 single, "Dark Horse," reduces symbols of

Egyptian culture and history—including mummies, cats, and snakes, all of which have religious significance—to mere visual spectacle and combines these with the racist appropriation of black culture in the United States (as Katy Perry dons cornrows and grills and travels in a lowriding vehicle with hydraulics). Most controversially, the video features a pendant inscribed with the Arabic word for God that is summarily engulfed in flames.

While mainstream music criticism has focused on the storm of public controversy—around the lyrics, referencing serial killer Jeffrey Dahmer; the copyright infringement case brought by Christian rapper, *Flame*; and the offensive religious imagery, which resulted in a viral petition with more than 50,000 signatures, (successfully) imploring the removal of a particular scene in the video—academic discourse has delved more deeply into issues of appropriation. Consider this 2016 essay by Rosemary Pennington, whose analysis of "Dark Horse" draws connections between cultural appropriation, Orientalism, and gendered capitalism:

*Figure 9.3* Katy Perry performing "Dark Horse" at Prudential Center in Newark in July 12, 2014

*Source:* Photo Credit Sleepyibis. Licensed under the Creative Commons Attribution 2.0 Generic license

*Dark Horse* is a visual feast . . . . [Perry] embeds nods to ancient Egypt throughout *Dark Horse,* frequently through her use of hieroglyphics as accessories. They appear on wigs, on Juicy J's (her *Dark Horse* collaborator) sunglasses, and floating in the air around a centrally framed Perry as she sings "So, you want to play with magic?" Perry's deployment of hieroglyphics, among the most recognized products of ancient Egypt, works to make the Egypt she's created seem less strange—most viewers will have seen hieroglyphics at some point in their lives—while the way she deploys them, as accessories, positions herself front and center. They, and the Egypt they represent, are meant to be consumed by Perry as well as by her audience. The nonlinear way the video is edited together, moving from barge to throne room, to a Perry surrounded by gold, floating hieroglyphs helps the audience navigate this strange landscape, latching onto what is familiar while allowing the unfamiliar to fly by. It works to create both an idea of Egypt, and an idea of an Egyptian Perry, as consumable; easily swallowed by viewers.

[. . .]

The destruction, transformation, and consumption of the Orientalist imaginings of men in *Dark Horse* exemplifies [. . .] that constructions of colonial otherness create objects of "desire and derision." We, the viewers, are meant to find Perry's annihilation of the suitors, her sporting of a glittery grill, and her wanton consumption amusing. The suitors are attractive, their presents are desired, but they themselves are nothing more than playthings at which we all laugh and then forget as the next victim, with his gifts, comes into view. A "brand of 'empowered' modern femininity" within capitalism is based on consumption that serves to reinforce patriarchy more than it serves to upend it. At the same time, Orientalism has informed a strain of Orientalist feminism that has helped construct "a binary opposition between a civilized West and an uncivilized East" (Ho, 2010, p. 433). It's a strand of feminism in which liberated White, modern, Western women know best and, much like their colonial predecessors (Hoganson, 2001; Woollacott, 1997), reinscribe Orientalist and racist understandings of difference instead of challenging them.

Perry, through her performance of an empowered woman who symbolically consumes Orientalized men one after another, is reinforcing a hegemonic understanding of the place of men and women in, specifically, capitalist society even though her consumption takes place in ancient Egypt. She is a golden winged, liberated, powerful woman who owes her position to her ability to consume all she can. Given the song's lyrics and the video's visuals, we are left with the expectation that Perry's hunger for things and for power is insatiable and that she will ride her dark horse into the ground to get what she wants, but she will do so by reinforcing heterosexist and Orientalist understandings of male and female bodies.[4]

This intersectional critique of the othering featured in Katy Perry's "Dark Horse" video is an exemplary instance of postcolonial music criticism, in that it highlights the colonial Western mindset and its appropriation of a misunderstood and misrepresented other.

## Postcolonialism and Critical Race Theory

As "Dark Horse" exhibits, Orientalism in mainstream popular culture is often infused with another form of othering: anti-black racism. In the history of the United States, the most pernicious othering was directed toward enslaved people forced from Western Africa to colonial America beginning in the sixteenth century. Although many of the principles of Orientalism and colonialism apply to anti-black racism, the conditions of African-descended people in the United States from the sixteenth century to the present day are so distinctive that a branch of knowledge—Critical Race Theory—emerged in the United States in the post-Civil Rights era to explore the ways in which laws, institutions, practices, and the media both condition and are conditioned by the construct of race.

### Race is a construct.

For most of the history of colonial America, race was understood through the concept of biological determinism. Biological determinism claimed that there exist divisions among humans that are hereditary, visible, and captured by racial designations, such as "black," "white," "Asian," etc. As the scientific community has confirmed, race is not biological; it is wholly constructed. There are no genes or gene clusters that are possessed by all people in a specific racial category and by no one outside of it. Greater genetic variation exists within groups labeled "black," "white," etc., than between them.[5] Indeed, skin color is no more meaningful than eye color as a marker of differentiation. Rather than a biological category, race is now widely understood as a symbolic category, based on physical characteristics and social and historical contexts.

Ethnicity, by contrast, refers to self-identified membership in a group based on cultural, historical, religious, and/or national affiliations. Ethnicity observes distinctions that are not acknowledged by the category of race. For example, ten Asian Americans might self-identify ethnically with Singapore, China, South Korea, North Korea, Japan, Indonesia, and

Cambodia. They might speak different languages, prepare different foods, and even have political conflict with each other. Nevertheless, they are all baldly categorized "Asian American."

**Racism is real, even though race is not.**

Although race is constructed, we still instantiate and perpetuate racism, perhaps most insidiously, by denying that it persists in contemporary society. In considering contemporary racism, Matthew Desmond and Mustafa Emirbayer articulated five pervasive fallacies about racism that frame (and confuse) public debate:[6]

*Individualistic Fallacy*

This fallacy assumes that racism exists in the hearts and minds of prejudiced individuals, rather than primarily in institutions, laws, policies, and practices from which all members of dominant society benefit.

*Legalistic Fallacy*

This fallacy assumes that racism can be (and/or has been) abolished completely and automatically by abolishing racist laws. Brown versus Board of Education provides an instructive example of this fallacy; although the groundbreaking 1955 ruling called for the legal segregation of public schools, redlining and unequal funding have continued to perpetuate segregation and unequal outcomes for people and communities of color.

*Tokenist Fallacy*

The belief that the presence of people of color in influential positions is evidence of the eradication of racial obstacles defines the tokenist fallacy. While the election of Barack Obama to the highest political office in the United States most certainly represents progress, it does not in any sense reflect the eradication of racism in our country, as articulated by the Black Lives Matter movement, which began during Obama's presidency to bring awareness to police brutality and racism.

*Ahistorical Fallacy*

It is sometimes argued that our racist history is inconsequential today; in fact, racist inequality is entrenched in our politics, education, employment sectors, and communities; and white supremacy still shapes the lives of people of color.

## Fixed Fallacy

The fixed fallacy purports that racism always looks the same and that it manifests in ways that are constant across time and space. From this perspective, the abolition of slavery and Jim Crow laws, for example, provide evidence that racism is in the past. In reality, racism does not always look the same from generation to generation.

Music is an instructive place to observe the persistence of these fallacies. Brad Paisley's 2013 country pop song, "Accidental Racist," exhibits each of the fallacies in Paisley's seemingly earnest but misguided attempt to engage with his internal conflict between "southern pride" and "southern blame." The song features a rapped verse by LL Cool J, in which, among other things, he equates wearing gold chains to being a shackled enslaved person.

In considering the lyrics further, we can observe the ahistorical fallacy, in Paisley's claim of implicit innocence for the crimes of the past. We observe the fixed fallacy, in his ignorance about the racist connotations of a scenario in which a POC waits on him in Starbucks while he wears a large Confederate flag on his T-shirt. We observe the tokenist fallacy, in LL Cool J's reference to "gold chains," suggesting material wealth. The individualistic fallacy is illustrated by LL Cool J's reduction of racism to "judging a book by its cover," and the legalistic fallacy can be observed in LL Cool J's expression of gratitude for the abolition of slavery. It is for these reasons that Ta Nehisi-Coates, writing for *The Atlantic*, concludes that "Accidental Racist" is really just "Racist."

> Paisley wants to know how he can express his Southern Pride. Here are some ways. He could hold a huge party on Martin Luther King's birthday, to celebrate a Southerner's contribution to the world of democracy. He could rock a T-shirt emblazoned with Faulkner's *Light In August*, and celebrate the South's immense contribution to American literature. He could preach about the contributions of unknown Southern soldiers like Andrew Jackson Smith. He could tell the world about the original Cassius Clay. He could insist that Tennessee raise a statue to Ida B. Wells.
>
> Every one of these people are Southerners. And every one of them contributed to this great country. But to do that Paisley would have to be more interested in a challenging conversation and less interested in a comforting lecture.[7]

Notwithstanding the importance of essays like Nehisi-Coates', music criticism is not solely focused on calling out racism in music and the music industry. An important alternative initiative is in giving voice to artists who fight for social justice. Writing for *Grimy Goods*, Patricia Sanchez highlights a powerful message by Bay Area R&B artist, H.E.R, whose single "I Can't Breathe" combines music and spoken word to situate the Black Lives Matter movement within the multi-generational legacy of racism in the United States:

> While it may be hard for some to put into words the anger, frustration or pain felt after witnessing the death of George Floyd, yet another innocent, black individual lost to a deep and systemic issue in our society, H.E.R. finds the strength and wherewithal to transcend her anger into a meaningful and eloquent piece of protest art.[8]

In another example, Joshua Barone, writing for *The New York Times*, highlights a creative production of Beethoven's opera, *Fidelio*, in which themes of freedom and justice are recast in the context of contemporary mass incarceration and Black Lives Matter:

> Beethoven's only opera, "Fidelio," is hardly a fixed text. He wrote several possible overtures for it and reworked the score substantially over the course of a decade. But its meaning never changed: the heroism to be found in devotion, love and freedom in the face of injustice.
>
> In 2018, the daring and imaginative Heartbeat Opera—an enterprise that, while small and still young, has already contributed more to opera's vitality than most major American companies—took the malleable history of "Fidelio" one step further, adapting the work as a moving indictment of mass incarceration.
>
> That production has now been revised for a revival that opened at the Grace Rainey Rogers Auditorium at the Metropolitan Museum of Art last weekend, ahead of a tour that continues through the end of the month. Already inspired by the Black Lives Matter movement, this "Fidelio" is now permeated with it, and the adaptation is even more powerful.
>
> In Beethoven's original singspiel—a music theater form in which sung numbers are set up by spoken scenes—a woman named Leonore disguises herself as a man, Fidelio, to infiltrate the prison where her husband, Florestan, is being held for political reasons. She aims to free him from execution while exposing the crimes of his captor, Pizarro.
>
> Ethan Heard, a founder of Heartbeat, adapted "Fidelio" for the company and collaborated with the playwright Marcus Scott on the new book. Their revision tells the story of a Black Lives Matter activist named Stan—sung by Curtis Bannister, a tenor of impressive stamina—who has been imprisoned for nearly a year, and whose wife, Leah, given

an affectingly agonized lower range by the soprano Kelly Griffin, is at a breaking point as she struggles to free him.

She gets a job as a guard at the prison; her strategy to reach Stan in solitary confinement (much as in Beethoven's original) is to ingratiate herself with a senior guard (here Roc, sung with both charm and dramatic complexity by the bass-baritone Derrell Acon) and court his daughter (here Marcy, smooth-voiced yet strong in the soprano Victoria Lawal's portrayal). In this telling, there is no need for the cross-dressing: Marcy and Leah are both queer. And, crucially, all of these characters are Black, a fact that looms before guiding the awakenings of Marcy and her father as they face their complicity in a racist system that, Leah says, is designed to punish "people whose only mistake was being poor and Black."

The spoken text is in English throughout, while the arias remain in their original German—a testament to the timelessness of Beethoven, though the production's surtitles take some liberties with the translation. (As an excuse for briefly letting the prisoners out into the sun, Roc sings that it's the king's name day, but the titles say that it's Martin Luther King Jr. Day.)

Radically transformed, too, is the score, arranged by Daniel Schlosberg for two pianos, two horns, two cellos and percussion, with the multitasking (and nearly scene-stealing) Schlosberg onstage, conducting from the keyboard. Expressive cellos reveal the characters' thoughts, and the horns add an aura of muscularity and honor. The most substantial interventions are in the percussion, with drum hits deployed to dramatic effect and a whiplike slap adding terror to Pizarro's murder-plotting "Ha, welch' ein Augenblick."

Not all the changes from 2018 were necessary, or wise. Starting with the venue: This production originated in a black box space at Baruch Performing Arts Center, which fit the chamber scale of the music and emphasized the cinder-block claustrophobia of Reid Thompson's set. At the Met, the show floats on an expansive stage and struggles with poor acoustics.

And the text has lost some of its grace, with pandering references to the Jan. 6, 2021, insurrection and President Donald J. Trump's infamous call for the Proud Boys to "stand back and stand by." A casualty of these lapses is the baritone Corey McKern's Pizarro, who is something of a Trump stand-in, a caricature among nuanced, human characters.

You could almost forgive that at "O welche Lust," the famous prisoners' chorus, still the emotional high point of the production and now a coup de théâtre. For the stirring number, Leah unlocks a chest—a metaphor for the prison gates—to release a white screen, on which a video is projected, featuring 100 incarcerated singers and 70 volunteers from six prison ensembles. The camera often lingers on individual faces, to an effect not unlike that of Barry Jenkins's filmmaking, the way his sustained close-ups invite intimacy and, above all, sympathy.

For curious audience members, Heartbeat has shared letters from some of the participants. They range from endearing—Michael "Black" Powell II's "German was hard!!"—to profound, such as this from Douglass Elliott: "Most of us are victims of our circumstances who when faced with adversities chose the wrong direction with our actions. This choir makes us feel that 'normal' feeling for a short time every week. We are accepted as humans, not looked at as numbers."

Beethoven's triumphant finale could have been an insult to the contemporary reality Heartbeat's production aims to conjure. So after Stan is freed and Pizarro defeated, Leah awakes at the same desk where, in the opening, she has had a frustrating phone call with a lawyer. This twist, that it was all a dream, is of course a tired trope, but what follows isn't.

After a moment of despair—her happiness felt so real—she stands, steps to a spotlight at center stage and holds up her phone, assuming the pose of her husband's activism, with which the production began. An ambivalent closing scene, it is an honest reflection of our time: of the mixed successes of Black Lives Matter, yes, and of the only possible way forward.[9]

As all of these examples illustrate, music is deeply entwined with the legacies of colonialism and slavery; music criticism, at its best, gives voice to social justice messages in music and educates audiences about music that perpetuates and instantiates inequality and racism.

### Chapter Summary

This chapter addresses two central questions as they pertain to music and its criticism: What is postcolonialism? What is critical race theory? The chapter analyzes examples of postcolonial and anti-racist music and then establishes central principles for music postcolonial and anti-racist criticism. The main points of the chapter are as follows:

- Edward Said's *Orientalism* explores the ways in which the non-West is constructed in the Western imagination. It focuses, in particular, on the implicit othering and the colonialist mindset in Western depictions of the non-West, broadly conceived.
- Said, along with Kamau Brathwaite, Gayatri Spivak, and others, has laid the foundation for postcolonial theory.
- Music can project, promote, or critique notions of self and other, right and wrong, strong and weak, West and non-West.

- Postcolonial criticism is concerned with how a work relates to and defines cultural difference, how "self" and "other" are defined and delimited, how power is wielded, and how resistance is understood and framed.
- Postcolonialism shares certain priorities and values with critical race theory.
- Critical race theory developed the post-civil rights era in the United States to respond to the unique circumstances of African-descended people living in the contemporary legacy of slavery.

## Guide Questions

1. How does Osmin's musical characterization in Mozart's *The Abduction from the Seraglio* relate to the political circumstances at the time of its composition?
2. Why is Katy Perry's *Dark Horse* considered to represent contemporary Orientalism?
3. How does Orientalism relate to anti-black racism in the United States?
4. Choose one of the fallacies of racism and find an example of its persistence in present-day music.
5. Explain biological determinism. Do you think theory persists today in some circles?

## Notes

1 Nicholas Till, *Mozart and the Enlightenment: Truth, Virtue, and Beauty in Mozart's Operas* (New York: W.W. Norton, 1995), 103.
2 This statement was made in a letter from Paul Gaugin to Vincent Van Gogh, Wednesday, September 26, 1888. BR. 1990: 694.
3 Edward Said, *Orientalism* (New York: Routledge, 1978), 11.
4 Rosemary Pennington, "Dissolving the Other: Orientalism, Consumption, and Katy Perry's Insatiable *Dark Horse*," *Journal of Communication Inquiry* 40, no. 2 (March 14, 2016): np.
5 Ian F. Haney Lopez, "The Social Construction of Race: Some Observations on Illusion, Fabrication, and Choice," *Harvard Civil Rights-Civil Liberties Law Review* 29, no. 1 (1994): 11–12.
6 Matthew Desmond and Mustafa Emirbayer, "What Is Racial Domination," *Du Bois Review: Social Science Research on Race* 6, no. 2 (2009): 335–355.
7 Ta Nehisi-Coates, "Why 'Accidental Racist' Is Actually Just Racist," *The Atlantic*, April 9, 2013, accessed July 10, 2024, www.theatlantic.com/entertainment/archive/2013/04/why-accidental-racist-is-actually-just-racist/274826/
8 Patricia Sanchez, "H.E.R. Shares Powerful New Protest Song 'I Can't Breathe'," *Grimy Goods*, June 23, 2020, accessed July 1, 2024, www.grimygoods.com/20 20/06/23/h-e-r-shares-powerful-new-protest-song-i-cant-breathe/
9 Jason Barone, "Review: Beethoven Returns for the Age of Black Lives Matter," *The New York Times*, February 14, 2022, accessed June 14, 2024, www.nytimes.com/2022/02/14/arts/music/heartbeat-opera-fidelio-review.html.

# 10 Music and Consumer Culture

As referenced in the introduction, renowned musicologist and music critic, Richard Taruskin, published a 2007 review in *The New Republic* that criticized classical music's most reverent audiences. In "The Musical Mystique: Defending Classical Music Against its Devotees," Taruskin argued that the preservation of classical music's highbrow status alienates would-be popular audiences from it.[1] He steps away from his traditionalist peers to argue that popular film can be a meaningful expressive backdrop for classical music; at the movie theater, audiences can enjoy classical music in all its glory without the highbrow associations and expectations found in the traditional concert hall. Whether by coincidence or not, many symphony orchestras have taken up this strategy for attracting audiences. New York Philharmonic's *Art of the Score* series, for example, has been running since 2013 and features a live symphony orchestra playing during a select film screening in an adapted theater/concert hall. Audiences and musicians alike are "electrified" by these experiences, in which fans "cheer so loudly as soon as the opening title pops up on screen, and we as musicians love that. We feed off of them and they feed off of us."[2]

Critics, it seems, are also enlivened by this partnership, which presents new dimensions of music and film to consider. For Ian gray, writing for RogerEbert.com, seeing *2001: A Space Odyssey* at Lincoln Center with a live score was "the ultimate trip":

> It was "Beatlemania" for adults. Avery Hall shook and rattled as the orchestra muscled through those famed, final chords to the crashing, exultant, living crescendo as "2001" pulled a full-blown Lazarus on that final tonic, and viola![3]

Gray went on to explain what exactly appealed to him about this pseudo-kitsch "middlebrow" collaboration, namely that "this event makes us engage with '2001' in anything but a passive, film student/viewer way":

DOI: 10.4324/9780429505171-14

*Figure 10.1* Boston Symphony Orchestra playing B52s at a Pops Concert
*Source:* Photo Credit Greg Suran. Licensed under the Creative Commons Attribution-Share Alike 4.0 International license.jpg

> Everything about tonight is lively.
> Everything about tonight is active.
> Even silence is something you *do*.[4]

There is no question that a primary benefit of this partnership between the symphony orchestras and film culture is the stream of diverse audiences flooding into the concert halls. An alternate and equally important stream, however, is that of revenue. Even organizations that produce art have bottom lines, expenses, and financial metrics. The orchestras' survival depends in large part on public support, concert revenue, donations, etc. As such, music is foregrounded as art all the while that it must be understood in the background as a commodity. Performances such as the one described above tend to draw larger and more diverse audiences than traditional symphonic programs do, making them an important part of a strategic business model for institutions such as the NY Philharmonic.

### The Case of Popular Music

Perhaps some lament the performances of *Angry Birds* themes and the *Harry Potter* score flowing out of concert halls, but the problem of music's cozy relationship to late-stage capitalism is not primarily located at the concert hall. It is primarily associated with popular music, and as a problem, it is not a new one.

Writing in 1941, after fleeing Nazi Germany in 1938, Marxist philosopher Theodore Adorno, wrote vehemently against the role of popular music in exploiting the masses and upholding the power of the elite and wealthy.[5] For Adorno, popular culture, and especially popular music, feeds people with debased anti-art that keeps them numb and politically apathetic. The popular culture "industry," as Adorno and his colleagues called it, produces unsophisticated, sentimental music and art that displaces the challenging and critical forms that might lead people to question their lives and their places in them. Though formulaic and standardized, "pseudo-individualization" makes this music appear differentiated through surface and incidental differences. For Adorno and his colleagues, the result is mass-produced, standardized, artificial music that pacifies rather than vivify; deadens rather than enliven.

Ironically, the subject of Adorno's intense criticism was jazz, which is now widely canonized as high art. Adorno was a member of the so-called Frankfurt School, a collection of Marxist philosophers based in Germany in the mid-twentieth century. They were concerned with the role of popular culture in exploiting the masses and maintaining the power of the bourgeoisie. For these scholars, culture had become something manufactured, something to purchase and passively consume, rather than something collectively and organically generated. According to Adorno, the appeal of popular music reflects and reinforces the deterioration of consumer taste in late capitalism. It works like this: The assembly line that produces the standardized automobile thus produces a numb, passive worker, who needs alternative stimulation (to that provided by meaningful, stimulating work). However, benumbed as they are, the worker has neither the inclination nor the capacity to struggle intellectually with true cultural artifacts; their entertainment must be simple and standardized, presenting only the illusory veneer of novelty. Popular culture fills this void with passive, pre-digested entertainment.

More recently, ideas like these have been taken up by George Ritzer, whose seminal *Mcdonaldization of Society* argues that the economic principles that govern the fast-food industry have come to dominate more and more sectors of society, including music.[6] The problem doesn't look entirely the same as it did in Adorno's time, but the challenges of producing and consuming music in late capitalism are familiar. Building on the social theory of Max Weber, Ritzer identifies four key principles that govern operations in the fast-food industry: calculability, efficiency, predictability, and control. Music, in Ritzer's system (like that food offered at McDonalds) is predictable, processed, and gratifying in the moment but ultimately not nourishing or satisfying in any enduring way. The purpose of this music is to earn money for the industry executives (labels and corporations) that own it, rather than to produce and reflect cultural meaning. For Seb Charleton, writing for the St. Andrew's *Saint*, Taylor Swift is similarly "the McDonald's of pop."[7] While conceding that a Happy Meal has its place in our culture, unlike Taylor Swift, we don't confuse it with Michelin-starred dining. For Charleton, Swift is a "chameleonic pop singer . . . hopping from trend to trend" in neat alignment "with the demands of the market." By example, Charleton points to the political turn in Swift's music—discussed in Chapter 8—which aligns with the legalization of same sex marriage (whereas her Bush-era music featured subtly disparaging references to the queer community.) Whether or not you agree with Charleton's reading of Swift's music and career, the music industry's participation in late-stage capitalism is undeniable. One particularly insidious example of music's commodification is in embedded advertising.

**Embedded Advertising in Popular Music**

Half a century ago, the lines between popular music and advertising were (more or less) clearly defined and delineated. A prominent agent in blurring those lines was hybrid rock/rap group Run-D.M.C., who created a relationship with the Adidas brand that conflated music and marketing, creating a hybrid form.

In the case of Run-D.M.C., however, the band's relationship with the brand developed organically. A staple of the band's style was Adidas sneakers worn without laces (as they would be worn in prison, where laces are prohibited). As D.M.C. recalls, a neighborhood doctor took issue with "felon shoes" and other attire of "thugs, drug dealers, and the low-lifes of the community."[8] The band pushed back, creating an album called *Adidas*, whose songs highlighted the positive aspects of their lives: "My adidas walked though concert doors, roamed all over coliseum floors, stepped on stage at Live Aid. . . . How you gonna look at us, not knowing you just said everybody wearing these sneakers . . . Don't you know I just stepped on stage at Live Aid? The people gave and the poor got paid." As history confirms, the album was extremely popular, and Adidas industry executives took note. When an L.A. industry executive attended a Run-D.M.C. concert, he witnessed 400,000 people in a sold-out Madison Square Garden concert hold up their Adidas sneaker while the eponymous song unfolded. The rest, as D.M.C. notes, "is history."

Importantly, in this example, the song plug preceded the commercial relationship. Since then, embedded messages, which feature deliberate, veiled commercial intent, reflect strategic economic relationships between brands and artists (or labels) that shape the music that artists create. (For example, the vodka brand, "Ciroc," is referenced in numerous songs by

P. Diddy, who is an investor in the brand and shareholder of the parent company, *Diageo*.[9]) One particularly problematic strategy employed by some advertising firms is to pay a fee to an artist for each airing of a song on the radio (or YouTube or other such site). This creates a low-risk opportunity for the brand, which only pays if the artist's song gets airtime; the artist, moreover, is incentivized to produce radio-friendly music with mainstream appeal. This practice is, of course, not unique to music. In many cases, when an actor drinks a Pepsi or opens a MacBook in the course of a film or television show, they are illustrating a strategic relationship with a brand that involves an economic exchange for subtle and subliminal advertising. Nevertheless, in the case of music—an artform that foregrounds and celebrates authenticity—embedded advertising can seem disingenuous or even manipulative. Artists themselves have sometimes taken the negative aspects of consumerism as their subject matter. In 2011, for example, Macklemore and Ryan Lewis released a stirring hip-hop ballad about society's insidious materialism through the example of a boy who wants expensive Nike sneakers so that he will fit in.

This musical critique of capitalism and its exploits, particularly as it preys on the poor and vulnerable, is nevertheless undermined by Macklemore's subsequent partnership with the NBA, which repurposed the song to promote the NBA All-Star Weekend in 2013. Given the NBA's close ties to Nike and the broader sneaker industry, it's not surprising that the commercial version of the song was stripped of all critical references to consumer culture. Indeed, the end of the commercial seems to endorse purchasing expensive sneakers in order to launch a successful career as an athlete. The hypocrisy of the song's repurposing did not go unnoticed, and after a surge of negative feedback, Macklemore offered a public statement, defending his choices:

> If you take away the consumerism cautionary core of Wings, a story still remains. And that story is one that I'm still proud of, and it's dope to me that it's relatable enough for TNT to want to use it.[10]

Macklemore's decision to commercialize his anti-consumerism message has, for some at least, undermined his music's broader social justice value. The reception of songs like "Same Love," "White Privilege," and "White Privilege II" is also impacted, despite the apparent earnestness of them. Indeed, selling a song about white privilege, thus further enhancing one's privileged status, presents analogous challenges.

For black artists, on the other hand (as discussed in Chapter 9), materialism can symbolize the shift within the black community from being an object of a pernicious form of capitalism to being a central subject. Ice Cube seemed to articulate all of this in the 1990s when he appeared, sampling his 1991 track, "Bird in the Hand," in a commercial for the high alcohol beer, St. Ides.[11] The song "Bird in the Hand" justifies the alternative lifestyle of selling drugs in terms of the systemic failures in our racist society to provide for the basic needs of most black Americans. As Eithne Quinn argues, by sampling this distinctive loop, immediately recognizable as "Bird in the Hand," in the commercial for St. Ides, which came out the same year, Ice Cube seems to be relating his new relationship with commodity culture—that is, making commercials—to the same survivor instincts that governed his earlier exploits.[12] The most insightful music critics and scholars navigate black artists' relationship to capitalism in relation to the racist history of this country.

## Music and Marketing in the Age of Social Media

This central challenge for artists, namely, to justly balance artistic and entrepreneurial motivations, hasn't changed over time; but the landscape in which this balancing act occurs has most certainly evolved. Social media, for example, has become a major and recognized force in negotiating the artistic and commercial success of musicians. John Herrman, writing for *The Quietus*, describes the sometimes outsized influence that social media has on an artist's career.[13] He begins with a vivid case example from Halsey:

> In a TikTok post last month, the singer Halsey shared a message with fans: "basically i have a song that i love that i want to release ASAP," the musician wrote, "but my record label won't let me." Despite eight years in the music industry and over 165 million records sold, Halsey said, "my record company is saying that i can't release it unless they can fake a viral moment on tiktok."

He next situates the Halsey example within broader industry trends:

> Several other artists had recently expressed similar frustrations with labels forever chasing the next "Old Town Road" or "Drivers License"— singles that took off on TikTok and climbed the Billboard charts. "All record labels ask for are TikToks," FKA twigs wrote in a since-deleted post on the platform. Florence Welch, Doja Cat and Charli XCX have also referred to their labels' TikTok fixations. (A little over a week after Halsey published the TikTok video, which became its own "viral moment," Capitol Records announced in a Twitter post addressing the artist that it was "committing to a release of 'So Good'" on June 9. "We

> are an artist-first company that encourages open dialogue," the label said in a statement. "We have nothing but a desire to help each one of our artists succeed, and hope that we can continue to have these critical conversations.")

While acknowledging the perennial issues of self-promotion for artists, Herrman situates the stories described above as conditions of a society online.

> Complaints from recording artists about promotional demands are as old as the music industry itself, and they have often played out in public feuds. But these recent grievances aren't targeted at the labels themselves. They are direct appeals to fans (in Halsey's case, 4.6 million of them on TikTok). And while they describe highly specific scenarios—world-famous artists in disputes with their labels over marketing strategies—they also evoke an experience familiar to just about anyone with a presence on social media, where aspects of the experience of fame have been formalized and made available to everyone.
>
> All of which is to say: Being told how to market yourself isn't just a celebrity problem anymore. It's a basic condition of being online.

Herrman goes so far as to cast contemporary pop stars as "de facto social media influencers":

> Some relish the chance to commune with fans online, and many found fame there first (including Halsey). Others are less enthusiastic, but understand that their fans—or their labels—appreciate an authentic online presence. All of this situates their complaints about TikTok within a more recent tradition: calling out social platforms.
>
> Like musicians, professional social media influencers sometimes find themselves at odds with their business partners. They, too, are under contract with large firms on which they depend for their livelihood and sense of self-worth, and which aren't shy about making demands.
>
> YouTube creators, for instance, depend on the platform for publishing, maintaining a relationship with their audiences, payment and distribution. For all but the largest creators, YouTube's management style is indirect. Its suggestions and demands are delivered, instead, through policies, extensive and frequently updated guidelines for creators, and direct prompts in its interfaces. Another way YouTube reaches its creators is through its analytics dashboard, which provides them with constant feedback from Google about how they're performing within the Google ecosystem.

Popular art has often referred to the conditions under which it was produced, and musicians' most dedicated fans have always gotten the picture one way or another—that their favorite artists are stressed about sales, or insecure about reviews, or unhappy with the conditions in their industry, or mad at their label. On YouTube, however, fans don't have to look for clues. Across the vast spectrum of YouTube content types, creators are frequently vocal about the job of being a creator on the platform. Subscription milestones are openly pursued and marked, and fans are routinely thanked—in direct and personal terms—for their support.

[. . .]

TikTok, which has quickly become a major cultural influence, is assertive even by industry standards. It's an environment in which users are subjected to constant nudges and suggestions about how to engage and what to post, one where complaints from famous artists about incessant marketing interventions don't sound so out of touch or unreasonable.

It's also an environment where folk theories of the algorithm abound, particularly about what it takes to show up on other users' feeds, known as "For You" pages. In a coming paper, the researchers Elena Maris, Hibby Thach and Robyn Caplan suggest that on TikTok, users have organized to draw attention to, and to try to influence, the opaque ways in which not just attention but actual money is distributed on the platform. (In December, TikTok introduced new monetization tools for creators, including a tipping feature.)

"With TikTok, we see this move from folk theories of algorithms to folk theories of compensation," said Ms. Caplan, a senior researcher at Data & Society, a nonprofit research organization. An awareness of TikTok's priorities—what it demands, and how it assigns worth—"is something that's seeping into the general population of users," she said.

In other words, visibility and self-promotion for artists are at once easier and more taxing than they were in the pre-internet days. Regardless, these are widely shared challenges in the ubiquitous realm of social media:

Millions of people can understand the tension of using Instagram with different potential audiences in mind (say, friends and family) or with a sense of professional liability (for instance, people who works for themselves, or in industries where a professional reputation is tied to an online presence). Noticing that your numbers are lower than usual and wondering what other people are doing that you're not are widely shared experiences, as is dismissing, or heeding, a recommendation about the newest feature or trend on a platform: Instagram Reels or

Close Friends; Twitter Spaces; YouTube Shorts; TikTok avatars. Haven't posted in a while? Expect a notification about it, or 20.

In 2022, you don't have to be a famous musician to get unwelcome recommendations from audience research, unsolicited instructions about how best to promote your brand, or regular updates on how many people are into your latest release. Joining a social network for personal reasons only to find yourself using it for material ends is, in fact, the standard experience. To bring it up, even as a world-famous recording artist, isn't just a bid for sympathy from fans on social media—in a small way, it's an attempt to relate.

This and the other stories in this chapter about music's complex relationship with consumer culture exhibit that there is no one right answer to questions about the balance between art and commodity. To be sure, an artist has to think strategically, and indeed economically, in order to have the means to create art (notwithstanding the romance carried in the image of the starving artist). At its best, commercial intentions can break down anachronistic barriers between highbrow and middle- and lowbrow cultures, as in a film screening of *Harry Potter* with a live symphony orchestra; they can expose the destructive impact of pernicious materialism on the health of communities and their members, as in Macklemore's "Wing$"; and they can highlight the systemic injustices that necessitate commerce outside of a system that fails whole identity groups, as in Ice Cube's "Bird in the Hand." As always, the critic's job in these instances is to explore and celebrate the innovation and collaboration that make artistic and commercial interests sometimes symbiotic; and to observe and chronicle the missteps that do harm to the consumers, fans, and the artistic community.

**Chapter Summary**

This chapter addresses the central question: How does music function in as a commodity in consumer culture? The chapter analyzes canonical examples of capitalist critique in music criticism and then establishes central principles of writing criticism that is informed and influenced by consumerism. The main points of the chapter are as follows:

- Capitalist critique is concerned with material culture and the power dynamics that support late-stage capitalism.
- Theodor Adorno was one of several twentieth-century philosophers to relate Karl Marx's political-economic ideas to music. He was deeply troubled by "predigested" popular music, which he felt transformed art into a commodity.

- Commodification and commodity fetishism may be seen as underlying many production and consumption patterns of contemporary music.
- George Ritzer recently developed a theory of "McDonaldization," in which he argued that the hyper-capitalist principles of fast-food production and consumption have come to dominant other sectors of society—including music. These principles are
  - Predictability
  - Control
  - Efficiency
  - Calculability
- Prominently, capitalist critics are concerned with whom a particular work benefits, how a work relates to commodity culture, whose economic situation a work projects and how class relations are symbolized in a given work.
- Social media may have an outsized impact on the public's experience and reception of music.

## Guide Questions

1. How does social media influence your musical tastes and listening habits?
2. Why is so much hip-hop focused on spectacular or hyperbolic consumerism?
3. Was Adorno's critique of jazz classist? racist? How is capitalist critique bound up with these other discourses?
4. Was Macklemore wrong to commercialize "Wing$"? Justify your response.

## Notes

1. Richard Taruskin, "The Musical Mystique: Defending Classical Music Against Its Devotees," *The New Republic*, August 2007.
2. Elysa Gardner, "A New West Side Story Experience at the New York Philharmonic," *Broadway Direct*, September 5, 2023, accessed July 18, 2024, https://broadway-direct.com/a-new-west-side-story-experience-at-the-new-york-philharmonic/.
3. Ian Gray, "Lincoln Center and Beyond the Infinite: *2001 Space Odyssey* with a Live Score Is the Ultimate Trip," *Rogerebert.com*, September 27, 2013, accessed May 20, 2024, https://www.rogerebert.com/features/the-art-of-the-score-film-week-at-the-philharmonic--2001-a-space-odyssey.
4. Ibid.
5. See especially, Theodor Adorno, "On Jazz," *Discourse* 12, no. 1 (Fall/Winter 1989–1990): 45–69.
6. George Ritzer, *The McDonaldization of Society: An Investigation into the Changing Character of Contemporary Social Life* (Newbury Park, CA: Pine Forge Press, 1993).
7. Seb Charleton, "Taylor Swift: The McDonald's of Pop," *The Saint*, December 2, 2023.

8 As quoted by Zac Dubasik in, "This History of Run-DMC and Adidas as Told by DMC," *Complex*, March 11, 2014, accessed May 24, 2024, https://www.complex.com/sneakers/a/zac-dubasik/this-history-of-run-d-m-c-and-adidas-as-told-by-d-m-c.
9 Ken Kurson, "The Real Reason Diddy's Arrest Matters," *The Observer*, June 23, 2015, accessed July 20, 2024, https://observer.com/2015/06/the-real-reason-diddys-arrest-matters/.
10 Macklemore, "Wing$, the NBA All-Star Game, & Selling Out," *Macklemore.com*, February 21, 2013, accessed June 22, 2022, https://macklemore.com/post/43688861186/wings-the-nba-all-star-game-selling-out.
11 Eithne Quinne, "A Gangsta Parable," in *Nuthin But a 'G' Thang: The Culture and Commerce of Gangsta Rap* (New York: Columbia University Press, 2005), 1–17.
12 Ibid.
13 John Herrman, "The Viral Spiral," *The New York Times*, June 24, 2022, accessed July 6, 2023, https://www.nytimes.com/2022/06/16/style/tiktok-viral-music-marketing.html.

# Part 4
# Critical Contexts

# 11 Album and Track-by-Track Reviews

## Album Review in the Age of Streaming

For many of us, the term "album" conjures an image of dusty crates lining the back wall of a thrift store, where hipster audiophiles hunt for rare vintage artifacts. There is no question that listening habits have evolved over the seven decades since the first commercial introduction of vinyl, and the concept of the album has changed along with it:

### Technology

Only a small minority of music is consumed on vinyl, the term most often associated with the concept of the "album." Notwithstanding the vinyl resurgence that has taken hold since the mid-two thousands, the vast majority of music listening today is digitally streamed.

### Economics

Streaming in turn impacts the way we think about album sales; the music industry widely uses the "album equivalent unit," a calculation that approximates would-be measures of album purchases for contemporary consumer listening habits. The Recording Industry Association of America (RIAA), for instance, uses a formula that equates 1500 streams to ten-track sales and (therefore) one album sale. Gold and platinum certifications are determined using these equivalencies, which reflects the move away from literal album sales.

### Artistry

Whereas, in the age of vinyl and (even more so) cassette tapes, technology encouraged a holistic listening experience through the course of a popular music album, today, albums are conceived on an experiential continuum, from the concept album on one end, which is created with a deliberate narrative arc, to a collection of unrelated singles, on the other.

DOI: 10.4324/9780429505171-16

*Figure 11.1* Circa 1970s Philips Turntable

In classical music, similarly, albums are not always intended to present a cohesive narrative journey. Indeed, one might come across an album consisting of Haydn's last four piano trios; those pieces are connected by instrument, composer, and chronology, though Haydn surely did not intend for them to be heard one after the other. On the other hand, Anner Bylsma's 2000 release, *A Portrait of Bach*, bookends a varied selection of J.S. Bach's music with two movements from his Brandenburg Concerto; in this case, order seems to matter, and the album is presented as a journey of sorts (though not a chronological one) through J.S. Bach's music.

Therefore, the first question to be answered when writing an album review is one of intent; namely, how is this music intended to be consumed? Does the album present a catalog of music from a specific time or on a particular instrument? Is it meant to be heard in one sitting? Is there a consistent theme or idea? Is there a narrative arc? In other words,

**The critic must first determine what holds the album together.**

In the case of classical music, the thematic structure can often be deduced, without extensive research, simply by examining the songs contained on it. For example, an album may comprise one large-scale work, such as Elgar's Symphony One, Beethoven's Symphony Nine, J.S. Bach's Mass in B Minor, or Haydn's *The Creation*. Alternatively, an album may by organized by instrument and/or genre, as in the Harp Concertos of Handel, Boïldieu, Dittersdorf, and Mozart; similarly, Murray Perahia's *Grieg/Schumann Piano Concertos* spans over 100 years of music that is nevertheless connected by instrument and genre. Sometimes an album will take on a bibliographic function by cataloging all (or much) of the music of a composer in a particular genre, such as Pinchas Zuckerman's *Beethoven Violin Sonatas* or Maurizio Pollini's compilation, *Chopin's Etudes, Preludes, and Polonaises*. Finally, disparate works may be paired to showcase the range of a particular performer/artist, as in Kyung Wha Chung's album, *Bruch's Scottish Fantasy and Mendelssohn's Violin Concertos*.

In the case of popular music, the critic must often deduce the thread that connects the album. *Tommy* by The Who tells a story about the titular character that unfolds over the course of the album; Taylor Swift's *Folklore* contains songs that are connected in mood, instrumentation, and style; Dave Brubeck's *Time Out* contains seemingly unrelated jazz standards that are nevertheless unified by their uncommon time signatures. *The Suburbs* by Arcade Fire reveals its thematic cohesion over the course of its songs, which chronicle generation X suburban youth as "Radiant with apocalyptic tension and grasping to sustain real bonds . . ."[1] For this critic it

> extends hungrily outward, recalling the dystopic miasma of William Gibson's sci-fi novels and Sonic Youth's guitar odysseys. Desperate to elude its own corrosive dread, it keeps moving, asking, looking, and making the promise that hope isn't just another spiritual cul-de-sac.[2]

And like a cul-de-sac, with its intentional circularity, *The Suburbs* ends with a reprise of the title song, "The Suburbs," undoubtedly nodding to the seminal concept album by The Beatles, *Sergeant Pepper's Lonely Hearts Club Band*.

Sometimes an artist offers clues to an album's intended meaning: Just three days after J. Cole announced the upcoming release of his surprise album, *KOD*, the rapper took to Twitter to confirm what the cryptic acronym stands for. He noted that *KOD* actually has three meanings: "Kids on Drugs," "King Overdosed," and "Kill Our Demons." In a follow-up message, he confirmed that he will explain nothing else: "The rest of the album I leave to your interpretation," he wrote.[3] This paradoxical offering and withholding of meaning provides fertile soil for the critic's interpretive work. Nevertheless, even when such clues are provided about the thematic structure of an album, a critic sometimes draws their own conclusions: Writing for the UK publication, *The Standard*, critic David Smyth emphasizes the overarching sound world of the collaborative release by Richard Dawson and Circle-Henki. Though the album is superficially unified by the quirky theme of extinct plants, what ultimately holds it together for this critic is the "bizarrely entertaining" sound profile of the album, to include "winding guitar lines and creepy whispering," unexpected turns and twists in the course of long breathed songs, contrasting vocals that combine mundane everyday poetry with singing "in the fictional language of the kingdom of Meronia."[4] In this clever review, the critic offers a new way of experiencing the album without contradicting the unifying features presented by the artists.

Next, the critic will

> **Establish a critical point of view that enhances the experience and understanding of the album.**

Many such points of view have been discussed and detailed in previous chapters. A critic may consider an album, for example, in relation to the artist's other work, as a cultural or political statement, or in relation to its genre or other related artists. As always, however, the central task of the critic is to point the reader toward the exercise of making meaning out of the music. Consider Christopher Weingarten's review of Andre 3000s Flute record, *New Blue Sun,* which he describes as "a breath of fresh incense." The essay begins by articulating what makes this album unique:

> There have been hundreds upon hundreds of ambient music albums released this year, but there's only one released by an elite-tier rapper with a 13-times-Platinum record under his overalls.[5]

The critic goes on to explain what makes it timely (and therefore also not so unique): "New Blue Sun also marks a peak in the decade-long crescendo of hipsterati new age revival." Unique or not, the value of the album, we learn, is in its sounds:

> Our bandleader has a wayfaring meander that dances in percussive bursts while his fellow players burble, simmer and sparkle. All these moving parts mean it's not exactly the most immersive environment for those seeking "calming" or "healing" music. However, when approached as the product of a tape-label basement jazz group or a subterranean electronic ensemble, New Blue Sun is an absolute joy.[6]

Finally, the critic places the album in an evaluative hierarchy within the canon, answering the implicit questions, should, and why should we listen to this?

> New Blue Sun is not the best ambient record you can hear in 2023 . . . . However, New Blue Sun will probably be the only ambient record many people do hear in 2023, and it's great that such a lively, sumptuous album gets the gig.[7]

As individual as this review seems to be, it nevertheless provides a useful template for album reviews:

1. Pull the reader in by addressing what is truly unique or exciting about the album under review.
2. Place the album in its genre or type.
3. Explore the album's sound profile in broad strokes.
4. Address the question of the album's value.

You'll note that this template avoids the sportscaster-style play-by-play (or song-by-song) discussion of the album; rather, the critic draws from key songs and moments to make a broader argument about the album's meaning and value. In general,

> Album reviews take a holistic approach to a work, highlighting specific moments in the service of an overarching argument about the album's meaning and value.

There is an exception to this rule of avoiding a chronological play-by-play, and that is in the track-by-track review.

### Track-by-Track Review

The track-by-track review is a popular format of music criticism in which the reviewer offers a brief, concentrated commentary on each song on an album. Despite the alternative format, the successful critic still draws connections among songs and conveys something about the album that is greater than its parts. Consider this review of Arcade Fire's fourth album, *Reflektor*, by Quietus journalist Julian Marszalek. The title track presents an opportunity for Marszalek to explore the sound profile of the album as a whole and its relationship to the band's previous work:

> [W]hat we have here is a stylistic shift for the Montreal ensemble that employs the production talents of DFA's James Murphy alongside long-term partner-in-crime Markus Dravs and marks a clear move to the dancefloor. Ushered in by undulating synths that give way to dance beats and a pumping bass, the track also highlights the talents of one David Bowie who is heard grinning around the five-minute mark. "Reflektor's" extended coda pauses to doff its cap to New Order before legging it with Peter Hook's bass riff from "Perfect Kiss" and transposing it to piano.[8]

Having established expectations for the album's sound profile, the review takes tracks as they come, both extending themes (of dance beats and '80s echoes) and pointing to defining features of individual tracks:

*Figure 11.2* Arcade Fire Live at the BUE Festival, Argentina, 2017
*Source:* Photo Credit Leonardo Samrani

**We Exist**

The move to the dancefloor is very much in evidence here courtesy of Billie Jean's four-to-the-floor beat that drives this track along. Slashed and reverberated guitars recall the work of Simple Minds before they decided they'd quite fancy having a go at being U2 and the throbbing bassline is rather worryingly reminiscent of Bon Jovi's paean to blue-collar life, "Living On A Prayer". And who said that mash-ups are a thing of the past? "Down on your knees/Begging us please/Praying we don't exist," sings Win Butler over the throb. But exist they do. We know because Butler tells us so. "We exist," he confirms. And it's in the song title.

**Flashbulb Eyes**

Fame, as a wise man once mused, puts you where things are hollow. And yes, the David Bowie influence is keenly felt on this meditation on the soul-sapping perils of a high public profile, specifically, his ill-advised flirtation with reggae circa *Tonight* and so it is that quite a few moves here are also cribbed from the mid-70s output from Jamaica. The deep bassline moves in and out of the skittering processed beats and electro drums while a Studio 1-type piano plonks away in the background while the overall track is drenched in reverb and echo.[9]

The critic here takes note of themes that are carried from song to song, encouraging a chronological listening experience:

### Here Comes The Night Time

Segueing from its predecessor, "Here Comes The Night" continues in the same musical theme but with more of an electro groove. Very much characterised by deep and punctuating keyboard stabs, tickled guitars and a piano break that attempts to ape the sound of steel drums, you almost feel threatened when Win Butler sings, "When we hear the beat from the street then they lock door." Bim![10]

Whereas an album review would focus primarily on unifying themes across songs, this critic takes advantage of the track-by-track format to highlight individual songs that stand out from the rest:

### Normal Person

Probably the most interesting track on the album, "Normal Person" is welcomed by the sound of concert crowd and a voice crying out, "Thanks for coming out tonight!" Once again, this is another groove based track underpinned by huge beats that also owes a debt to Bowie's *Lodger* thanks to a snaking guitar line that Adrian Belew would be proud of.[11]

Subsequent track reviews present a similar combination of unifying and differentiating themes, as described below:

### Awful Sound

Latin-type rhythms soon give way to gliding strings and slashing chords before a wave of processed beats take over. Cinematic sweeps are certainly at play here before yielding to a middle-eight that moves the track into a more drone-based territory. But then, just as you think you'e got a hang of this thing Arcade Fire then make a sharp left turn and swerve into the lush area of pop balladry.

And then, unlike most of the other tracks contained here, it comes to a sudden halt.

### It's Never Over

We're back to the 4/4 beats again with a number that sounds like New Order commanding a tank battalion in the Battle Of The Bulge. This owes much to dance music in the broad sense as drops are deployed throughout before being blasted away by the kind of bassline that Peter

Hook probably hums whilst waiting for his pizza to come out of the oven. And it certainly goes on for long enough and in the process it sounds as if Arcade Fire are remixing themselves as they go along. "It's over too soon!" they sing at the end. They're lying.[12]

While the last track on the album presents an opportunity for holistic reflections on the journey, this critic stays true to the track-by-track format, focusing on the sounds and meanings of this particular song; only implicitly are we invited to reflect on this as an ending (in which the listener is "sent to bed without any supper"):

### Supersymmetry

Clocking in at a wopping 11.17, this is a meditation on mortality as Win sings, "I know you're in my mind/But it's not the same as being alive." Arpeggiated synths are stabbed with bass and the track slowly starts to build up, up, up and you're expecting the bomb drop or just simply something to happen but sadly nothing does. Except for the six-minute coda wherein an inexperienced pair of hands are seemingly let loose on a harmoniser before having it taken away from them and then sent to bed without any supper.[13]

The track-by-track review format may be better suited to albums with only loose connections among the songs. An album with a strong narrative arc or sense of cohesion may be better served by the album review format.

## Writing for a Specific Publication

A final consideration in writing an album or track-by-track review concerns the publication that a critic is writing for. There's no question that the mission, style, and perspective of a publication will shape the musical works that are reviewed in it; however, sometimes an album or piece of music has crossover appeal and is reviewed for multiple, disparate audiences. Consider, for example, Keith Jarrett's release of 18 sonatas by Carl Philipp Emanuel Bach, the son of J.S. Bach. Keith Jarrett is best known as a world-renowned jazz musician, notwithstanding his numerous solo and classical piano concerts and recordings. A classical album release by a prominent jazz musician has significant crossover appeal, and publications devoted to both jazz and classical music thus justly reviewed this release. The tone and substance of those reviews reflect the perspectives and voices of the different publications. For example, Karl Ackerman, writing for the online publication, *All That Jazz*, highlights the improvisatory character of the younger Bach's compositions, pointing to their suitability to Jarrett's expertise in jazz improvisation. He finds in Jarrett's performance "a deep respect for these multifaceted scores' improvisatory, animated nature."[14] Ackerman concludes that "[m]ore than many of his classical projects, these compositions align with Jarrett's exploratory nature; an erudite use of counterpoint and meter, and effortlessness in the adaptation of classics for a modern audience."[15]

Azusa Ueno, writing for *The Classical Review*, has a different response to Jarrett's recordings of the C.P.E. Bach Sonatas. For Ueno, Jarrett's recording, while featuring moments of "delicate transparency" and (elsewhere) "assertive robustness," on the whole lacks urgency and drama. Continuing, he assures us that

> [t]he want for more drama isn't entirely the pianist's responsibility but also that of the medium itself. Mahan Esfahani's recording on harpsichord (Hyperion), for instance, sounds totally different: there is much more rhythmic definition in his phrases and the plucked timbre is crucial in adding necessary vitality.[16]

Because these C.P.E. Bach sonatas were originally composed for harpsichord, this critic, reflecting the Historically Informed Performance (HIP) movement discussed in Chapter 2, hears the modern piano as anachronistic. This critic faithfully represents the values of the publication's constituents: classical music listeners have, on the whole, been socialized to prefer historically informed performance practices, and the Jarrett performance on piano violates this most important virtue. Listeners of jazz, by contrast, look for improvisation and experimentation, which was the emphasis of the previous review. As this example illustrates, a successful critic writes for a specific audience and from the perspective or the publication at hand.

## Chapter Summary

This chapter discusses the album and track-by-track review, provides illustrative examples, and offers practical tools and exercises for writing for these media. The main points of the chapter are as follows:

- The length, tone, and even content of an album review are shaped by the particular publication for which it is written.
- The critic should conduct research on the publication and get to know its audience, voice, and perspectives.
- The critic may listen to the album in the following ways:
  - As a sound world
  - As a narrative

- As a set of discrete tracks
- In relation to the artist(s)'s other work
- As a cultural or political statement
- In relation to its genre or category
- In relation to other related artists

- In general, critics should avoid the "sportscaster, play-by-play" style of review and focus on the attributes of the album as a whole.
- The track-by-track review is distinct from album review and requires a different critical approach.
- The negative review should be approached with respect and care.

**Guide Questions**

1. Choose an album review of a musical work that you know well. Copy and paste the first and last paragraphs into a separate document and write your own version of the inner paragraphs. Compare your review to the original.
2. Choose a track-by-track review of a musical work that you know well. Copy the first and last track reviews into a separate document and write your own version of the other tracks. Compare your review to the original.
3. Write a short album review as if it were for two completely different publications. Choose the publications in advance and write your pieces to reflect the mission and voice of each of them.

**Notes**

1 David Marchese, "Arcade Fire, 'The Suburbs' (Merge)," *Spin*, August 11, 2010, accessed June 14, 2022, www.spin.com/2010/08/arcade-fire-suburbs-merge/.
2 Ryan Pinkard, "Arcade Fire: A Decade of Decadence and Danceability," *Tidal*, March 30, 2015, accessed March 22, 2021, https://tidal.com/magazine/article/arcade-fire-us/1-11700.
3 Rania Aniftos, "J. Cole Confirms Threefold Meaning of Upcoming Album 'KOD'," *Billboard*, April 19, 2018, accessed October 22, 2021, www.billboard.com/music/rb-hip-hop/j-cole-confirms-meaning-kod-album-8357007/.
4 David Smyth, "Richard Dawson & circle-Henki Review: A Bizarrely Entertaining New Sound World," *The Standard*, November 25, 2021, accessed November 16, 2021, www.standard.co.uk/culture/music/richard-dawson-and-circle-henki-album-review-b968104.html.
5 Christopher Weingarten, "André 3000's Flute Record Is a Breath of Fresh Incense," *Rolling Stone*, November 20, 2023, accessed May 1, 2024, www.rollingstone.com/music/music-album-reviews/andre-3000s-new-blue-sun-review-1234886904/
6 Ibid.
7 Ibid.

8 Julian Marszalek, "Arcade Fire's *Reflektor* Reviewed Track by Track," *The Quietus*, October 15, 2013, accessed June 22, 2023, https://thequietus.com/articles/13607-arcade-fire-reflektor-review-track-by-track
9 Ibid.
10 Ibid.
11 Ibid.
12 Ibid.
13 Ibid.
14 Karl Ackerman, "Keith Jarrett: Carl Philipp Emanuel Bach," *All That Jazz*, June 15, 2023, accessed July 12, 2024, www.allaboutjazz.com/wurttemberg-sonatas-keith-jarrett-ecm-records.
15 Ibid.
16 Azusa Ueno, "Double Review: C.P.E. Bach—Keith Jarrett, Einav Yarden," *The Classical Review*, July 7, 2023, accessed September 21, 2022, https://theclassicreview.com/album-reviews/double-review-cpe-bach-keith-jarrett-einav-yarden/.

# 12 Program Notes and the Live Concert Review

**Program Notes as Guide**

A friend of yours has a spare ticket to a concert one evening at the NY Philharmonic. You ask them what is being performed and learn that there are (at least) a few pieces on the program that you'd like to hear. Having accepted the invitation, you grab a quick bite from a street vendor after work and walk (while eating) the seven blocks to the symphony hall. Upon arriving, you shuffle through the doors where you exchange your ticket for a concert program and find your way to your seat. Glancing at your watch, you note that the concert should begin in about nine minutes. You open your program and begin to read.

What would you like to learn in these nine minutes before the concert begins? This is the fundamental question that the concert program seeks to answer. Historically, some of the most significant program notes were written by a work's composer to guide the experience of listening to non-representational (instrumental) music. In fact, an entire genre of symphony emerged in the nineteenth symphony, called the programmatic symphony, in which a written statement by the composer accompanied the performance of a symphony in order to shape and guide the listening experience. In 1845, Hector Berlioz provided a particularly renowned example of this genre in his *Symphony Fantastique*. The five-movement instrumental symphonic work was accompanied by the following notes:

> The composer's intention has been to develop various episodes in the life of an artist, in so far as they lend themselves to musical treatment. As the work cannot rely on the assistance of speech, the plan of the instrumental drama needs to be set out in advance. The following programme* must therefore be considered as the spoken text of an opera, which serves to introduce musical movements and to motivate their character and expression.

DOI: 10.4324/9780429505171-17

*This programme should be distributed to the audience at concerts where this symphony is included, as it is indispensable for a complete understanding of the dramatic plan of the work. [HB]

### Part one

#### Daydreams, passions

The author imagines that a young musician, afflicted by the sickness of spirit which a famous writer has called the vagueness of passions (*le vague des passions*), sees for the first time a woman who unites all the charms of the ideal person his imagination was dreaming of, and falls desperately in love with her. By a strange anomaly, the beloved image never presents itself to the artist's mind without being associated with a musical idea, in which he recognises a certain quality of passion, but endowed with the nobility and shyness which he credits to the object of his love.

This melodic image and its model keep haunting him ceaselessly like a double *idée fixe*. This explains the constant recurrence in all the movements of the symphony of the melody which launches the first allegro. The transitions from this state of dreamy melancholy, interrupted by occasional upsurges of aimless joy, to delirious passion, with its outbursts of fury and jealousy, its returns of tenderness, its tears, its religious consolations—all this forms the subject of the first movement.

### Part two

#### A ball

The artist finds himself in the most diverse situations in life, in the tumult of a festive party, in the peaceful contemplation of the beautiful sights of nature, yet everywhere, whether in town or in the countryside, the beloved image keeps haunting him and throws his spirit into confusion.

### Part three

#### Scene in the countryside

One evening in the countryside he hears two shepherds in the distance dialoguing with their "ranz des vaches"; this pastoral duet, the setting, the gentle rustling of the trees in the wind, some causes for hope that he has recently conceived, all conspire to restore to his heart an unaccustomed feeling of calm and to give to his thoughts a happier colouring. He broods on his loneliness, and hopes that soon he will no longer be on his own . . . . But what if she betrayed him! . . . This mingled hope and fear, these ideas of happiness, disturbed by dark premonitions, form the subject of the adagio. At the end one of the shepherds resumes his "ranz des vaches"; the other one no longer answers. Distant sound of thunder . . . solitude . . . silence.

*Part four*

March to the scaffold

Convinced that his love is spurned, the artist poisons himself with opium. The dose of narcotic, while too weak to cause his death, plunges him into a heavy sleep accompanied by the strangest of visions. He dreams that he has killed his beloved, that he is condemned, led to the scaffold and is witnessing *his own execution*. The procession advances to the sound of a march that is sometimes sombre and wild, and sometimes brilliant and solemn, in which a dull sound of heavy footsteps follows without transition the loudest outbursts. At the end of the march, the first four bars of the *idée fixe* reappear like a final thought of love interrupted by the fatal blow.

*Part five*

Dream of a witches' sabbath

He sees himself at a witches' sabbath, in the midst of a hideous gathering of shades, sorcerers and monsters of every kind who have come together for his funeral. Strange sounds, groans, outbursts of laughter; distant shouts which seem to be answered by more shouts. The beloved melody appears once more, but has now lost its noble and shy character; it is now no more than a vulgar dance tune, trivial and grotesque: it is she who is coming to the sabbath . . . Roar of delight at her arrival . . . She joins the diabolical orgy . . . The funeral knell tolls, burlesque parody of the *Dies irae*,\*\* the *dance of the witches*. The dance of the witches combined with the Dies irae.

\*\*A hymn sung in funeral ceremonies in the Catholic Church. [HB]

A contemporary performance of Berlioz's canonical symphony would surely include the artist's statement, above, but today's concertgoer may want other information as well. Time, though, is limited, as articulated in the fictional characterization of the concertgoer at the beginning of the chapter. For this reason, I particularly like the program notes published by the San Francisco Symphony Orchestra for a 2017 performance of Berlioz's *Symphonie Fantastique*.[1] The program is organized with headings that include basic information about the work (e.g., Duration, Instrumentation, US Premiere, and Recent Performances); background information about the work and composer (titled, The Backstory); a description of the music, which includes an annotated version of Berlioz's written program; and a list of notable recordings and further reading about the piece. Scanning this well-organized program, the reader can choose to focus on aspects of the work and performance that interest them most. Relevant information is easy to find, and yet at under 2000 words, one can read the entire program in an average-length intermission.

Perhaps most importantly, this program contains the most useful and relevant information about the work and avoids elaborating on scholarly nuances and other details that don't enhance the enjoyment of the live experience. It begins with a compelling and well-chosen background story. (Indeed, who doesn't enjoy a good love story?):

> On September 11, 1827, Berlioz went to the Paris Odeon for a performance of *Hamlet* by a company from London. The younger female roles were taken by Harriet Smithson, a twenty-seven-year-old actress who had been brought up in Ireland. Berlioz fell instantly and wildly in love with her.[2]

As the vivid account continues, we learn that the violence of his feelings for her and her repeated rejections provided the creative momentum for this great work. As we move to the section about the music, this background information provides valuable context for engaging with the work's sound and structure. In the unfolding discussion of the music, the critic annotates the composer's own words with pointed remarks that highlight audible features of the music, thus enhancing the listening experience:

> the sound of the muted strings, the unmeasured pauses between phrases, the single pizzicato chord for violas and cellos, the two strange interventions (also pizzicato) for the basses, the mysterious cello triplets rocking back and forth at the first climax, the one appearance of flutes and clarinets with horns. What an amazing effect it is at the end of the slow introduction when the chord of winds with tremolando strings is hushed, then swells again, like music carried on the whim of capricious winds.[3]

These words are clear, compelling, and tied to audible features of the music. The best program notes, like this one, combine the past and the present, positioning the contemporary listener as a part of history in the making.

### Live Review

Whereas program notes are generally read from one's seat in a concert hall, the live review is more often found in the newspaper at the Sunday kitchen table. As such, the live review has multiple audiences: the first audience is the one that will use the review to decide whether or not to attend the concert. This audience is looking for an evaluation of the concert as well as a sense of the fittedness to their tastes and preferences. The second audience will not attend the concert and reads the review for its own sake. (Most of us will never go to Burning Man; forewent Taylor Swift's Eras Tour, etc.) For this reader, the review is its own aesthetic experience, analogous to attending a concert. Its primary functions are to entertain, edify, and/or uplift the reader through the vicarious experience of live music. The most successful reviews cater to both audiences; they tell a story about the concert that can stand both beside a concert and in place of it. Consider the following live review of a Pulp concert, published in *The Quietus*. Neil Kulkarni's review of the reunion festival concert of Pulp begins with a broad and general commentary on the festival scene. Not only do these opening remarks capture the pre-concert setting and mood, they serve to legitimize our critic, with references to other related bands, the critic's anti-consumer philosophy, and even suggestions of their own noble struggles for their art. In these remarks,

*Figure 12.1* Pulp performing at the Isle of Wight Festival, 2011

**The critic presents their credentials and earns our trust.**

> I've avoided festivals for nearly 15 years now, avoided the live-music explosion that now so proudly is the real money-maker for the music-biz, avoided all the reunions, repackaging and remastering of my youth, resisted the irresistible lure of my favourite bands playing the same old shit they played when I first saw them. Not to do with principles, I would've loved to have seen Pixies and Pavement for example. I stayed out of it mainly because I've been too poor a punter to see any of it. But there is this, too, the branding that hits you as the cattle come through the gate and Barclaycard Wireless Festival bring you this stun-gun to the temple, this Nintendo cocktail bar, this Live-nation VIP grandstand, this Jagermeister shot-bar, this gnawing sense that you're in an out-of-town leisure-plaza. Be grateful and be happy 'cos that's an order right from Huey Fun Loving Criminal on the big screen. He's got a Barclaycard too.[4]

This critic also knows that:

**A live concert is much more than music.**

Thus, the story begins hours before the event:

> So far so harrumph. BUT I'm here squinting at the sun just off Marble Arch because even my grouchiness can get broken. Even I can live in hope again. In two hours Pulp are going to be on stage and I can't think about anything else. Some bands get back together and you're happy for them, wish them luck on their bank-raid, wave the fizz-swilling party out to the waves forlornly from the shore of your skintness, rattling your bottles in Rollocks Yard all the way home to watch it on You-Tube instead. Pulp I wasn't gonna miss. Pulp I had to see. Couldn't live through a year knowing they'd played and I hadn't been there. The kids can starve this summer and my arse is taking Barclaycard's short and scalys up to the hilt. Because if any band can rise above, just like they always did, then it's Pulp, if any band can remind you that music transcends commercial taint and transports you into another way of life, another model of living, then it's Pulp.
>
> Yes I'm here chasing memories. But I'm also hoping for a reminder of hope. The whole day my skin is tingling, my heart is pounding, time lagging and then catching up with itself in crazy moments of blurred acceleration, every side-street a memory and every snicket a regret.[5]

Though one might expect a chronicle of the concert itself to follow this preamble,

**The concert review need not unfold chronologically.**

On the contrary, whereas the actual event unfolds steadily from the tailgating pre-concert experience to the jammed parking lot at the end, the review can fast forward, skip, and rewind as much as the author pleases. In fact, the author can leave the time frame of the concert altogether, taking the reader through a time machine to the band's beginnings, previous concerts, and/or other relevant events, before moving through the evening in, or out of, order. You'll notice that this review doesn't unfold as a play-by-play. On the contrary, time shrinks and stretches (and bounces around):

> Weird old journey down from Cov, driving down Holloway Road through Archway, remembering parties, times where you could hitch to the smoke with nowt but your pretty face and still survive, still end up on a friendly floor or pitch up arse-about-tit on the pavement. Those London balconies, those mattresses and those regrettable fumblings, those pills and powders, those long nights of longing and laceration, happiest days of my life when I didn't have to worry about getting up in the morning, and could start every day not knowing where the hell I was.
>
> 15 years on, I park my car at Euston, stroll past benches I once kipped on waiting for the 5.30 am train back up to Cov, take a long leisurely stroll down Tottenham Court Road, the shock of the missing Astoria, the angry rush of Oxford Street, a smoke and a wettened whistle on Soho Square and then onward to the park.[6]

Time travel provides a vivid journey to the critic's youth and, through that, to the band's beginnings.

> London's a city that immediately brings Pulp and the 90s vividly back to me, the still-resonant conviction that in an era draped in the flag, at a time where independence was being turned into a orthodoxy, Pulp uniquely were OUR band, for OUR people. In a pop world where other bands were trying so hard to be your heroes or your heartthrobs Pulp were like your mates, and knew that your mates and you were all the stars you needed. Like your mates, an odd bunch, ageless, sharp, like your mates shot through with a thread of genius that stood out in the crowd and drew the eye. OUR band, that repaid belief longer than the Manics or Suede ever did, alongside Pram as true poets of that age, but writing pop-songs and blessed with a front man too good not to occasionally take over the mainstream they provided such withering counterpoint to.

> In an age when the dumb and clever-clever were being propounded as our only alternatives, Pulp were about real street-level intelligence and guile and survival and they gave us songs that spoke like we did about the messes we got ourselves in without any jazz-hands smarm or monkey-walk lairyness. They delineated our first loves, our lingering decay, our furies and our freakouts and our dance-steps, the cuts of our jib and our clothes, helped us to know we weren't alone standing off to one side, scowling on the stairs, waiting moodily for their songs at the edge of Britpop's dancefloor, conquering it every time 'Lipgloss' hit. Their songs were so much better than anything else, so naturally, effortlessly, breathtakingly superior in sound and word and stance.
>
> The last time I saw them was also in a park in London, Finsbury in 1997, and it was perhaps the only time (this side of Public Enemy or the Muses) in my gig-going life where I'd felt proud to be part of the mass, proud to call myself one of the many, because it felt like a glorious calling-together of the Pulp nation, the Pulp tribe, it felt like going to see Pulp was a political act, an act of bravery and courage in a sea of rock & roll gestures and retrograde rearranging.
>
> Stella supped, roach ground out, wobbliness definitely setting in, let's see if we can belong to something bigger than ourselves again, let's go *rejoin* the Pulp collective and see how gracefully we've all grown up. I bet the bastards look better than I do.[7]

Returning to the present, the critic surveys the crowd; the reader follows along as if watching through a GoPro:

> Today's crowd out front is not really a crowd. It is a group of people united only by a shared ticket purchase and a shared box of chips, eaten while huddled on the dusty ground (five quid). And, have to say, they don't LOOK like Pulp fans. Where are the Nancy-boys, the anti-girls, the tall drinks-of-water and the little geeks? They're all wearing shorts and sandals and can afford the goddamn food and are gonna sing along with "Common People" then go home and hate chavs. I'm feeling a trifle disconnected, a feeling I fear won't dissipate all night. For how can I feel connected with these people anymore? They're not my friends. They have their own friends. Pulp is all we now have in common and I don't think they need them as much as I did and do.
>
> I look around and I see all the things that have become associated with festivals, all the things I find impossible to know are real or not. Cowboy hats, dancing like a hippy, aviators, denim shorts, beach balls, whoops, phones aloft—are these things to do or things we do at the rock show now, expected behaviour waiting for an emblematic moment on the big

screen from the swooping crane? So often seeing gigs recently I can't help thinking that in these Guitar Hero, TopShop Ramones-t-shirt years all we've been doing is playing at stuff, bands PLAYING AT being in bands, audiences PLAYING AT what it means to see a band, behaving in a way as predictable and unspontaneous as the ghastly phrase 'party like a rock star' demands.[8]

At last, the critic turns to the music. They set expectations, pulling us into their sense of anticipation:

> Pulp themselves of course had presentiments of this: *This Is Hardcore* is a whole album about how pleasure can play itself out, how those zones and centres of joy can become dry and arid through saturation, just how middling the highs and lows can become. So I find myself, holding my breath, wondering whether this show is for me and mine or everyone here, realising that no one here is lost, no one here is tripping the fuck out, most of us have work in the morning, everyone here is hoping that their entertainment dollar has been well spent as the clouds gather, the sun hides, and a message travels across the black sheet that obscures the stage. "Do you remember the first time?" We've changed so much since then, we've grown. Apart from each other.
>
> But. Hold the phone. There he is. There they are. Here is "First Time". All is whole. Pulp are still a deeply political act of listening and love. First thing that needs noting, my god how fucking brilliant do they sound? A band that's played together long enough to click in each other's pockets and on the one straight off, never making a show of that rock solid togetherness, able to be six individuals yet part of something bigger than any single personality.
>
> Senior's violin has taken on a beautifully Cale-esque droning pall, slightly off-tune, Candida marshals the full palette and pushes it to all the right peripheries, keyboards and string swelling with a symphonic strength bigger and louder than I've ever heard them before. And my god Banks, Webber and Mackay are still such a fucking amazing thump of electric wow, coiling round The Voice, attendant to every syllable, enacting high-wire drama and low-life luridness with a pan-optic blast that seems to fill the sky fresh every second.
>
> And of course, thank god, Jarvis is still perhaps thee greatest British lead-singer we've had in the past 20 years, sharp, bearded but beautiful, chatty, funny, serious, utterly believably *still bound up in these songs* and the memories and moments they evoke, not just for us, but for him and his band. So it doesn't matter that the set mainly focuses on *Different Class*—these songs were universal and timeless to begin with, hearing them now, in the new contexts of both our age and his, they actually

sound more lethal than ever, cast an even harsher light on the piddling pleasantry the post-Pulp age has mainly given us.[9]

At this point, the critic narrows their focus to detail specific songs:

"F.E.E.L.I.N.G.C.A.L.L.E.D.L.O.V.E." thunders with drama and heart, "This Is Hardcore" blazing in red-lit Portishead-style doom and danger, "Underwear" and "Mile End" ushering in a beautiful sunkissed few minutes of bliss but smuggling pipebombs and prophylactics in the rear of your ear lyrically, reminding you how uncomfortably close to home, how voyeuristic Pulp always felt. OUR band. OUR problems. OUR only solution—by the time "Mishapes" comes I'm remembering just how much that song held me together back in the day, how it still holds me together now, goggling at how Banks and Cocker have an almost Mick'n'Charlie knowledge of each other's moves (loved it when Jarvis started intoning Shelley's Adonais like Jagger in 1969), what a glowering still-fearsome presence Senior is in the sound. "I Spy" and "Bar Italia" are delightful surprises, "Es and Whizz" still perhaps the greatest song of its era, everything played with a full-tilt perfection a million miles away from mere reanimation—these songs have grown since then, now stand mighty amidst the dwarfed mediocrity of modern indie pop, put out with a power and beauty that only seems to have increased with age, a dignity that feels immortal.

That's what's startling, how a "reunion" show can actually reunite all those lost threads, bring something back full-force, can actually make you realise what you've been missing, how missed the majesty that is Pulp has been for so long. On a pulsating "Disco 2000" and a riotous "Babies" they're actually, impossibly, even BETTER than I remember them, somehow heavier yet freer, more precise yet even funkier (and they always were a bad-assed band to dance to). Couple of really revealing moments—one when he mentions the student protests and how crucial education was in bringing Pulp together, one where he talks about the new billionaires development at the bottom of Hyde park (placing us neatly in between the recently-closed St Martin's College and Cameron's new Britain)—where the politics comes to the fore, and you're reminded, heartbreakingly, of just HOW FUCKING MUCH WE NEED A BAND LIKE PULP AGAIN in the current shitstorm, just what a big gap they left when they went, just how unprepared the modern audience has now been conditioned to be (both statements barely get a round of applause) for a band with something to fucking say.

I can't see a thing but I can hear, and that's all that matters to me, that I'm here and in the same place where this righteousness and romance is erupting. And it doesn't matter that I'm disconnected from the crowd, because the best Pulp always reminds me that in family and in friends and in solidarity there's a way, a stylish rather than merely fashionable way, to stay sane, to stay good, to stay true. "Common People" is deeply telling tonight. Almost no-one here is living a life with no meaning or control, most of the crowd are singing along with "Common People" 'cos it might just get them through, but some of us remember, and know in Cameron's new age how close that drift and derailment is no matter how grown up we might think we are, no matter how secure we think the emergency credit being advertised on all this branding is.

Crucially it's still a song that divides, that knows, that calls you out, that's still murderously accurate, that still showcases what a truly great resistant voice Jarvis Cocker and Pulp have been in English pop. OUR band. Still like our mates, a bit grouchy with each other, but still in love with each other and what they can create together. The band least likely to do something new together, but the band I would most like to be back in the fray.[10]

Finally, the show is over, but the review is not:

My voice has gone, my body aches, I have just been jumping up and down and screaming for an hour and a half. I have a routine to get back to. But for 90 minutes in a field in central London Pulp have made me happy again, made me believe that despite pop's ongoing self-censorship and refusal of possibility, its glee in its own pimping and dumbing down, there are still people able to take the form as far as it can go, to say things fearlessly, to try and create a heaven on earth, right wrongs, fight the good fight.

I have next to nothing to say about 2011, and very little to say about pop anymore but I do know this: it's not all about the music, it's not all about the fans, and it's not something that corporations have a fucking clue about. This much I know because I am a fan. Despite the enforced commercialism, the Styrofoam and the big-screens and the smarming security, while Pulp are on tonight nothing else in the world matters other than those six people under the big black sky and what happened in the space between them. Back in the game. Selling one of the kids to get tickets to Brixton because tonight was a groundshaking reminder that where Oasis bequeathed condescension and Blur bequeathed caricature, Pulp, more than any other 90s group, gave us compassion, something entirely different, something to live your life by, something that can sustain you. All hail.[11]

To be sure, this review is not a concert per se, but reading it is an experience in its own right. The critic takes the reader on a multi-sensory journey that includes the tingles before the show, the wobbliness from too much debauchery, the attire of people crowding the seats, and of course the music entering the ears (and body and mind). The reader, in turn, experiences a journey that, while not the same as attending a concert, elicits many of the same emotions: anticipation, reverie, joy, meaning-making. While not all live reviews have the character of this one, the best of them do share with this the vivid storytelling, sense of anticipation and arrival, the extramusical details that live concerts offer, and the sense of collective meaning and shared experience that live music can provide.

## Chapter Summary

This chapter discusses the concert program and concert review, provides illustrative examples, and offers practical tools and exercises for writing for these media. The main points of the chapter are as follows:

- The purpose of the concert program is to provide background information and guide the listening experience of the audience.
- The critic should research the repertoire, conductor (concert master, bandleader, producers, etc.), performers, audience, and venue.
- Most concert programs are written for a general audience.
- The live review is about the live experience in addition to the music.
- The live review need not unfold chronologically.
- The live review shapes the reader's expectations of the event and/or may provide its own aesthetic experience.

## Guide Questions

1. In what ways is a concert program different from a live review? In what ways is it similar?
2. Should a critic approach a live review differently from an album review? Why or why not?
3. Choose a concert on YouTube or, if possible, plan to attend a live event. Conduct research in preparation for the event, attend the concert, and write an 800–1200 word live concert review, using the principles outlined in the chapter.

## Notes

1 Michael Steinberg, "Program Notes: Berlioz: *Symphonie Fantastique (Fantastic Symphony: Episode in the Life of an Artist*, in Five Parts), Opus 14," *San Francisco Symphony Orchestra*, September 2017, accessed September 18, 2021, www.sfsymphony.org/Data/Event-Data/Program-Notes/B/Berlioz-Symphonie-fantastique.

2 Ibid.
3 Ibid.
4 Neil Kulkarni, "'Still a Deeply Political Act of Listening & Love': Pulp Live," *The Quietus*, July 6, 2011, accessed October 16, 2021, https://thequietus.com/articles/06542-pulp-live-review.
5 Ibid.
6 Ibid.
7 Ibid.
8 Ibid.
9 Ibid.
10 Ibid.
11 Ibid.

# Index

Adele 10, 78–79, 84, 101
Adorno, Theodore 156, 162, 163
Aleatoric Music 63
Allyship 132, 134, 138
*Alternative Artifacts* 64
Anderson, Laurie 5
Arcade Fire 69, 169, 171–173
audience 4, 9–11, 14, 28, 42, 43, 49, 53, 83, 99, 102, 118, 146, 155, 182
authenticity 134, 158

Bach, J.S. 25, 28, 30, 38, 50, 51, 168, 174, 175
Bartels, Jeff 66
The Beatles 32, 33, 58, 59, 74, 137, 169
Beauvoir, Simone de 130
Beethoven, Ludwig 5, 24, 25, 29, 56, 65, 89, 89, 118, 119, 150–152, 168
Berio, Luciano 56–58, 65
Berlioz, Hector 89, 90, 178–181
Beyoncé 120
Bowie, David 32, 130–131, 171, 172
The Byrds 43, 45

Camp 131–137, 100
capitalism 13, 14, 41, 49, 50, 145, 146, 155–162
Carroll, Noël 11, 14, 107, 108, 109
castrato 38–39
Citron, Marcia 118
colonialism 142, 147, 152
Critical Race Theory 13, 130, 147, 153
criticism 2–5, 9, 10, 14, 15, 69, 89, 100, 106

Debussy, Claude 3, 56, 57, 65, 86–88, 94, 96
Dujardin, Filip 46–47
Dylan, Bob 32, 41–45, 49, 83, 120

EDM 9, 18, 36, 60, 130
embedded advertising 157–158
Eminem 48
entertainment 9, 65, 84, 85, 99, 104, 105, 156, 186

fallacies of racism 153
folk 41, 43–45, 49, 104, 161

genre 2, 10, 11, 25, 35, 36, 44, 45, 48, 50, 53, 58, 60, 61, 80–84, 94, 95, 96, 169, 170, 171, 178
Gill, James Francis 61
globalization 48, 50
Golijov, Osvaldo 58–60
Guerrilla Girls 113–114

harpsichord 26, 27, 32, 34, 36, 42, 75, 175
Hegemann, Helene 53
Hendrix, Jimi 118
H.E.R. 150, 153
Hip Hop 36, 45–51, 119, 134, 158
historically informed performance (HIP) movement 26, 175
history 4, 5, 9, 12, 13, 16, 25, 30, 32, 34, 39, 40, 41, 45, 49, 52, 56, 57, 65, 80, 81, 128, 137, 138, 145, 147, 157, 181
Holiday, Billie 39, 58, 79, 81
Hongzheng, Han 122–123
hooks, bell 116, 120
hyperreal 46–47

Ice Cube 45, 158, 162

Joplin, Janis 120, 121

Kant, Immanuel 6, 7, 17

Lamar, Kendrick 39, 46–50
live music 78, 182, 182–189

Macklemore 133, 158, 162
Mahler, Gustav 56, 57, 65
Marx, Karl 13, 156, 162
McCartney, Paul 32–35
McClary, Susan 118, 119
McDonaldization 156, 163
McLeod, Kembrew 45, 46, 49
#MeToo Movement 89, 92, 116
Micah, Elephant 44–45
Minaj, Nicki 12, 73, 119, 120
Mona Lisa (La Giocanda) 21–25
Mozart, Wolfgang 10, 26, 27, 60, 80, 102, 106, 141–143, 169
Monet, Claude 86–87
Moreschi, Alessandro 38–41

Nakhane 127–129

Ocean, Frank 134–137

patriarchy 113, 119, 127, 129, 146
Perry, Katy 1–3, 10, 32, 37, 45, 132, 144–147
Pitchfork 44, 106
plunderphonics 61, 62

Post Truth 63, 64, 66
Pulp 182–188

queer theory 12, 128, 130, 139

racism 48, 116, 147–152
Reich, Stephen 60
Ritzer, George 156, 163

Said, Edward 12, 142
Schiele, Egon 69, 70, 71, 73
Schumann, Clara Wieck 117
Shakespeare, William 7, 42, 139
Stone, Carl 62, 63
subjectivity 6, 7, 17, 88
Swift, Taylor 11, 94, 95, 132–134, 157, 169, 182
*Symphonie Fantastique* 89, 181

Taruskin, Richard 9, 154
taste 5–9, 15, 81, 107, 156, 163, 182
technology 28, 35, 37, 39, 42, 45, 54, 62, 78, 167
Thicke, Robin 88–89
TikTok 159–161

Varese, Edgard 77

Wagner, Richard 4, 80, 81
Weber, Andrew Lloyd 98–99
Willis, Ellen 120

Zedd 35
Zeppelin, Led 107